AN INTRODUCTION TO

Spiritual
Ecology

THE MAGIC OF NATURE

MARIAN GREEN

ROBERT HALE

First published in 2022 by Robert Hale, an imprint of
The Crowood Press Ltd
Ramsbury, Marlborough
Wiltshire SN8 2HR

enquiries@crowood.com
www.crowood.com

British Library Cataloguing-in-Publication Data
A catalogue record for this book is available from the British Library.

ISBN 978 0 7198 3154 6

Cover design: Blue Sunflower Creative

Typeset by Simon and Sons
Printed and bound in India by Parksons Graphics

CONTENTS

CONTENTS

DEDICATION AND ACKNOWLEDGMENTS

I dedicate this work to Mother Nature who has sustained me throughout my life.

I would like to thank my friends who have been such a support during the last seventeen months, especially Bee, Mo and Kim. I thank Fawziyah for her leaf drawings, and my many friends and relatives, far and wide, who have always been there at the end of a phone for me.

I would also like to thank The Crowood Press for their patience and encouragement during this drawn-out process.

May the Holy Ones bless you all.

Marian Green, Bristol, Lammas 2021

Preface

Our world is undergoing many changes; some on a small, local level, others on a planet-wide scale. Over the years many of these have been positive and controlled, and have brought benefits to health, quality of our food and safety of the world around us. Now, however, there are powerful forces for transformation that seem to be bringing chaos and disruption to many. When a situation occurs beyond our control, and beyond our wildest nightmares, many of the certainties by which we live our lives get swept away. From the ruins of our previous 'normal' existence we will have to lay new foundations, arrange new plans and rethink many aspects of what we are doing and where we want to go. The viral infection called Covid 19 that swept through the world in 2020 irrevocably changed people, especially those affected by the millions of deaths around the planet. Continuing ripples of ill-health may continue into the future until effective and widespread vaccination and other remedies are available.

Everywhere people realized they could work remotely, at home, saving time and money on draining commutes to their places of work, or perhaps change what they did for a living. Some were inclined to move house to have more space for a home office, or a garden to cultivate. Of course many suffered, being forced to stay in, spend more time with family members or those who depended on them, not always to their benefit. Some people who lived alone, or were isolated from loved ones, friends or colleagues, were greatly affected by this. A proportion of those who caught this infection also suffered long-term complications – although the newly developed vaccines and new therapies have restored freedom to many.

As well experiencing separation and upheaval, many people began to re-examine what really mattered to them. When shops were closed it was necessary to use what was already at hand, and the continual chore of buying more things became less important. This need to possess more, have new items or accrue extra clothes and so on may have caused some people to reconsider the whole matter of owning less. Some people did all their shopping on-line and found returning to physical shops in person quite strange, and have continued to get groceries and other necessities delivered to their doors.

Among these shifts of perception is the growing need that humans should reconnect with Nature. By ignoring the state of the Earth beneath our feet and all the countless living things around us, we have allowed the transformation of the land, the waters, and the use of precious resources to be over-used. Now many are waking up to this situation, or being shaken by the drastic change in weather patterns, animal extinctions and pollution that are caused by us. Everything is connected, the Earth, the many life forms, from microbes to huge elephants and whales, from plants to people. We are all parts of the web of existence and if one part is damaged everything, animal, mineral and plant, is affected.

We are created from star-stuff, evolved and changed by time. Evolution has given us many gifts, but it also gave humanity free will, and some of our activities are now known to be destructive, harmful and polluting. In the twenty-first century we are reaping some of the dark harvest our species has sown.

Spiritual Ecology

Spiritual Ecology is a concept that has evolved from a wide array of different streams of experience and so is difficult to define. It is based on an individual's relationship with the natural world and so is unique to them. It is connected to so many threads of human life and experience – history, Nature, science, religion and some aspects

7

of actual magical practice. Many people are involved in it in one way or another. The definition came about when someone asked me how I described myself. I said, 'I am a Spiritual Ecologist.' And the concept stuck.

For many years I have worked with real magic, the power of Nature, the traditions of the past and the wisdom of countryfolk. I feel connected to legendary and fictional wizards like Merlin, Gandalf and J.K. Rowling's Professor Sprout. All these characters were well-read and learned, yet *practised* what they had learned. Nature is magical, and magic is natural, a series of skills that can be mastered.

Today the wise don't have to battle dragons so much as unseen adversaries or bureaucracy. It is essential for everyone to have less screen-time and more green-time. We have become Nature-deprived and lost our inherent magic. We can't google the taste of strawberries or read how the wind in our hair feels; we have to actually experience these things, explore and learn.

This book is intended to be a ramble through many vast subjects, for the power of Nature is felt everywhere from the minutest living thing to the wide extent of the cosmos. All are part of the whole, and each entity can influence the others. Many things can only be touched on briefly here because the list is endless; it is timeless, eternal and infinite. Each seeker will have to find their own meandering path while following their individual quest. This process is not easy, it is not fast, but it is utterly fascinating and life-enhancing. An aspect of our lives that has recently been transformed is the realization that no one is impervious to the effects of Covid 19, severe weather and natural disasters. For some people, this has awoken a new spiritual awareness. Spirituality is a path of choice, the individual searching for our soul's path and a personal revelation of the meaning of life. It has few of the limits of an organized religion, introduces no priesthood, no book of rules between the Creator and creation. We can move forward on our own paths, bound by common goodwill, and ethical behaviour. We do not need to see the stars in a picture in a frame; we can see the stars with our own eyes in the night sky, so they can inspire and guide us. So it should be with Nature – a personal experience for us and especially our children, bringing connection and fulfilment. Through direct contact with the natural world, our spiritual path will bring us closer to health, happiness and contentment.

Magic and the Universe

Although the arts of magic are ancient, the concepts behind their techniques are very modern. Today's science talks of many dimensions of space–time, whereas the esoteric world speaks of planes of existence. The realms our awareness enters in dream and visionary states may well be attempts at consciously entering other dimensions, time lines or states of being.

Originally people lived closely with Nature, using what they found around themselves, eating wild food and being aware of the Sun and Moon, and the changing seasons. As time has gone by we have become more controlling, more artificial and more distant from the natural world. Now the separation is being seen as creating all sorts of drastic results, from our changing climate, to our mental, physical and spiritual health. It is recognized that we, as dwellers on planet Earth, need to do something before all these problems become insurmountable. One of the possible ways of alleviating some of this pending disaster is to take personal action.

If we, as inhabitants of the Earth can look to becoming guardians, instead or parasites, we may be able to make positive changes. We can learn to improve our relationship with the planet, respect Nature, recall the aspects of people's past that brought harmony rather than conflict between Nature and human nature. We may be a part of the problem, but we can surely also be part of the solutions. We can renew our positive links with Mother Earth, respect her seasons and the gifts of fertility, stability and nourishment, for body, mind and spirit. We can become 'Spiritual Ecologists', drawing on our ancestral magics, our endless creativity and our desire for change for the better. There is a lot to do.

What Needs to be Done?

Every effort needs to be made to prevent lost generations of young people growing up with no knowledge of or connection to the natural world. Some schools are able to take their pupils to camps, city and country farms and to visit the countryside. It is encouraging to hear about the development of 'Forest Schools' for young folk and even the Japanese concept of 'Forest Bathing' for people with little opportunity to envelop themselves in the wilderness. Any kind of outdoor experience is so valuable. Learning about growing things, about birds and wild animals, insects and bees, butterflies and ladybirds, enriches the soul.

None of these activities costs money, but rather the spending of time on spiritual exploration and adventure. It may seem difficult to see that looking at a wild flower will offer a connection to the Creator but if these simple adventures don't happen, there can be a spiritual void.

Accruing physical things because the media indicates they are essential to a happy life, having sexual encounters without love and affection, drinking alcohol or taking drugs 'for recreational purposes' are not soul-enhancing activities. Unless young people have opportunities and guidance to expand their awareness, their world will contract to a small flashing screen, artificial images and ear-deadening music. Each baby has the whole cosmos before him or her, wondrous arrays of places to explore, animals and plants to learn about and a huge variety of foodstuffs to taste and enjoy. If children aren't encouraged to try a wide variety of fruits, vegetables and freshly cooked dishes, it is more likely that they will turn to familiar fast food or tasty snacks. Everyone needs nourishment, not artificial flavours which are sweet, sugary, salty and ultimately addictive. These fast foods also come wrapped in plastic, which all too often is just casually thrown down anywhere. Any kind of addiction will harm physical health, and many harm mental acuity and spiritual progress. They are literally soul-destroying.

In this book many traditional ideas about Nature and sustaining our relationship with the green world may be explored. We can all rebuild or extend our connection to wild places, to trees and stones, to plants and animals, to rivers and oceans, and to the tides and cycles of our ever-turning planet. We can restore the ancient magical arts which have guided people since the Stone Age, learn to heal ourselves and perhaps others, and through this help to heal the Earth. By respecting life we can develop a modern spiritual impulse that honours the past, works with change and creates hope for the future.

This will be no easy task; it will require a new outlook on the way we live, and what we use and consume. There are no instructions set in stone, no list of 'Dos and Don'ts' but common sense will help you take steps towards a brighter future, shared with all living things that dwell on planet Earth.

By becoming more aware of the problems and discovering what tiny steps each person can take, change will happen, gradually and gently. It may take a hundred years to grow an oak tree, ten years before a new fruit tree is productive and a season before many flowers and vegetables are ready. Patience is one of the first skills to learn. Time is not wasted while we wait for something to happen; most of us need to slow down, turn off the intrusive electronic chatter and feel the wind, appreciate Nature in all her aspects, or watch the patterns in the clouds above our heads. These things bring inner calm and clarity of purpose, and from such a still centre comes creativity and healing. Waiting is not wasting time, it is an opportunity for meditation and reflection.

PART I

RECOGNIZING THE NEED FOR A SPIRITUALITY TODAY

1

WHAT IS SPIRITUAL ECOLOGY?

There are many paths within the realms of spiritual awakening, including the major religions. All have a tradition of wisdom, but some have become dominated by men and reliance on written books. Priests and Priestesses should be teachers and guides inspired by their connection to the Creator and to Nature.

Another overlooked spiritual path is that of magic, which was often a part of orthodox faiths, which relied on Divine inspiration, mystical healing powers and the working of amazing miracles. Today magical arts can be used to help and to heal, whether it is an individual or the whole planet. We are part of Nature, we have human nature, and through this link, with experience and patience it is possible to bring ourselves to a happier state and to do something beneficial to the planet we live on. This is no easy task, it is complicated and a huge responsibility, but as the saying goes 'If not us, then who? If not now, then when?' To take small steps to understand our own part in the pattern of creation, to understand our own needs, the skills we have or can develop, our links with the eternal, perhaps seen as the ancient Gods and Goddesses of Nature, can be genuinely effective. The field of knowledge of the natural world and its history, and the traditions of magic, contains a vast amount of data. There will be countless things to learn, to try and to discover on this journey of spiritual ecology, getting to know ourselves, and the aspects of Mother Nature with which we can interact. It is an endless quest.

We are living in a world where most of our physical needs can be met, yet many people still feel they are missing something, something which is hard to define. It is a sense of yearning that is seldom discussed with friends or family, nor often shared in social media or thought about most of the time. Perhaps it is because we have somehow lost our ancestral connection to magic, the power of Nature, or our inner spirit. Schools do not teach the arts of awareness to the subtle senses we possess, nor the ability to recognize the value of intuition, the stillness of meditation and common sense. Today religion seems either to follow authoritarian rules, with many 'Thou shalt nots...', a wishy-washy pattern of hymns and prayers, or a very strong, book-led form of instruction as to how life should be. In the last few decades various aspects of Paganism have become widely publicized, and people have been drawn to Wicca. This has led some to covens under the guidance of High Priestesses, in order for festivals to be celebrated based on the Turning Year, and the worship of both Goddesses and Gods, often drawn from ancient pantheons. Other people have followed a solo path, like traditional wise folk, or share their celebrations with friends or family. There is no Book of Rules, but rather ethical concepts such as 'Do no harm but follow your true will'. This sounds simple, on the face of it, but knowing your 'True Will' can be a lifetime's work. It is not greed, nor is it necessarily need, but a deep impulsion to act for the best of the world.

We Each Need to Find our Own Path

Each of us has to find our own spiritual direction; there is no one book, no fixed set of guidelines. It has to come from the heart, through meditation and exploration of our own feelings. You do not have to believe in specific Gods or Goddesses, worship in a particular place or at a particular time, or celebrate festivals and events, unless you want to. It may be that you recognize that you are born of star-stuff, but created, shaped and nourished by planet Earth, seen by some as Mother Nature.

You may come to understand that the Sun in the sky, which gives us day and night and the seasons of the turning year, has traditionally been acknowledged as a God, or in some Northern traditions, a Goddess. It might be that the Moon, whose ever-changing face, time of appearance and region of the sky is always shifting, might be a Goddess, or sometimes, according to ancient Egyptian belief, the God Thoth. Perhaps by reading or by thinking about what you believe now, or have been taught, your understanding changes. If you choose to follow a Pagan or an orthodox religious path, then you will have personal experiences or sources of wisdom that can alter your point of view.

To see a spiritual direction that is linked to Nature and the world around you will require you to experience that world. Not through reading or electronic information, but by venturing into a park, a garden, the sea shore, a wood or another wild place. You will be going there, no matter how briefly at first, to learn about other aspects of the living landscape, and of hidden parts of your own being. You do not need to tread this way alone, if you have friends or family members who will share your journey. It might take courage to go somewhere different, to do things outside your normal range of activities, like sitting silently under a tree, or just exploring your own feelings, but what you come to sense will be very fulfilling. Even exploring a supermarket fruit and vegetable aisle to try something new puts you in touch with a small aspect of the natural world.

Many aspects of practical magic involve ideas that may seem new to you, but often they will cause you to recall things you used to know. Most people will have had experiences that have left strong, positive memories, perhaps of holidays by the sea, or in beautiful countryside at home or abroad. Sometimes these were so thrilling or impelling that they were uplifting or 'spiritual'. Two things usually are involved in this intense feeling; one is doing something different or new, and the other is that often they are out of doors. Certainly beautiful buildings, exquisite pieces of art or uplifting music can induce such moments, as can human love and affection or sudden inspiration, but in order to reawaken a spiritual aspect of life involving magic, it has to be looked for and controlled.

Tread Lightly on the World

The arts of magic are very ancient, but they can be learned with patience and practice. The ultimate objective of magic and Nature spirituality is to make the practitioner a better person. One of the first concepts to recognize is that nothing and no-one is perfect. Examine the leaves of a plant – each one will differ slightly from another. If you compare two of the same plants, they will vary in shape or flower pattern. Each is unique, as are you. You don't need to compare yourself to anyone else, but just to strive to be the best, kindest and most positive person you can be. Pagan faiths are based on happiness, not guilt, They are designed to free adherents from restrictions, but still have the concept of 'Do as you would like others to do to you'. An old magical motto states 'I seek to know in order to serve'. The greater your knowledge, the greater your ability to help yourself and others. One of the things in greatest need, which magical actions can help, is the Earth herself.

A lot has been written in recent decades about our need, as humans, to tread more lightly on the planet we share with billions of other life forms. We really do need to take notice of the science of climate change – not just opinions, but hard facts. Nearly everywhere on Earth is experiencing extreme weather events. We may not be able individually to prevent pandemics, floods, tornados, wildfires, droughts and melting ice floes, but we can be aware of their consequences, reduce our own use of precious resources and begin to consider magically what we are doing. It may seem trivial that we should each try to act consciously in all we do. Many magical arts of divining and healing require the practitioner, whether witch, wizard or Nature guardian, to actually see what is around them, hear the sounds of the world and eventually sense other mystical energies which surround and support us.

This awareness of life around us is what spiritual ecology is about. By not just recognizing details of the physical environment, but sensing the deeper aspects or energies you can learn to draw on positive magic. There are a number of basic exercises that need to be mastered which will help you connect with these unseen powers. The arts of magic concern change, so it is important that you can tell what is changing if you are trying to influence something. Being aware of what is affecting you now will give you a basis to alter it, understand it or use it to enhance your inner self. Often the first exercise is that of meditation, a mental and physical stillness, with a relaxed body but an alert mind. Like many aspects of this work it sounds easy, but it does require patience and practice.

The Importance of Meditation

Western meditation does not require the body postures of yoga, nor chanting mantras, burning incense or candles. It can be done anywhere reasonably quiet, where you have a supportive chair to sit upright on. Place your feet flat on the floor, or a support if necessary, with your hands on your lap. Breathe steadily and slowly, relaxing every part of yourself. Close your eyes. Listen to any sounds. Do they distract you? Can you feel tenseness anywhere? Gently let it go. Allow your muscles to relax. You can't make this happen, you have to let it happen. Silently tell yourself that it is good to be still and peaceful. Feel a sense of balance and mental emptiness. Let your thoughts drift, focusing only on taking slow deep breaths, down into your belly. You could count to eight breathing in, hold your breath for a count of four, breathe out for eight and hold that for another four. Work out a speed of counting that suits you, even using the beat of the pulse in your wrist, while looking inward at your own sense of peace. Soon you will be able to hold a calm, poised state of being. It might not happen at once, but be patient and persistent.

The ancient skills of magical practice are not mastered in a few minutes or hours. You may find you need to keep quiet about this process because some people pour scorn on things they don't understand, and any comments can be hurtful and off-putting. Be patient until you are able to sense a change in your state of awareness. This is essential to magical work, but it helps in real life too. Being calm and focused will help you discover your true will.

Other senses which you may need to awaken are those of imagination and wonder. You can begin to do this by looking at a real flower. It is grown from the Earth, yet its petals are not the colour of earth. They may be red, blue, white, yellow or purple. Its leaves are green. Think about the transformation that has happened since a seed germinated, to grow and produce the plant you are looking at. Think about the forces of Nature that turned water and minerals into the shapes and colours you see, and also the scent you can detect. Each flower, each blade of grass and every tree is a kind of miracle, brought about by a combination of Nature and time. Allow yourself to feel a sense of awe at what happened to create that plant.

Look at the sky, notice the clouds, and see if you can discover forms or faces in their shapes. Sense the air you breathe, the solid ground beneath your feet. These are all physical experiences which form the basis of real magic. As you permit yourself to notice these natural things, your sensitivity will increase, and in time, your magic will be more powerful.

The ancient arts are not the wand-waving, immediate effects of fictional witches and wizards, but the outcome of years of determined practice that builds into the mental and spiritual toolbox of an effective practitioner. Wonderful things do happen quickly, but usually after a long period of preparation. You can achieve many of the things you wish to do, but it will require hard work. There is no such thing as a free hunch! You need to develop sensitivity, feel what is really happening, and find out how that can be improved. You will also have to examine your desires, your motives, your life situation and relationships with those around you. You should try to get out of doors as much as you can, for this will lift your spirits and enhance contact with the healing forces of Nature.

The Age of Aquarius

Some of the concepts of modern Pagan religion emerged in the 1960s when many young people were looking for alternative life-styles. It was seen as the 'Dawning of the Age of Aquarius', although from an astrological point of view, we are on what is called the cusp between the ages of Pisces and Aquarius.

For thousands of years sky-watchers have observed the patterns of stars in the night sky, especially those in a band that appears to encircle the Earth. In that band there are twelve major groups of stars, or constellations, that form the basis of the Zodiac, whose name in Greek means 'The Wheel of Animals'. Every day the Sun moves across this background of the stars of the Zodiac, taking around thirty days to cross a single sign, which indicates our 'sign of the Zodiac' in astrology according to our birthday. The Earth and the planets move around this at different rates, and their positions have been recorded in tables of an Ephemeris, from which astro-logers would derive information to cast a horoscope. However, the Earth is tilted on its axis with a slight wobble, so that over thousands of years the stars don't exactly line up with where they used to be. Every 25,500 Earth years, which is known as a Great Year, they get back to the starting point which in our calendar is the Spring Equi-nox at the beginning of the Zodiac sign of Aries. This phenomenon is known as the 'Precession of the Equinoxes'.

The Ephemeris used by astrologers is different from the Sidereal Ephemeris used by navigators. The Sidereal, or 'starry', Ephemeris records the *actual* visible position of the Earth against the stars. For the last 2,000 years or so, the Spring Equinox has actually shown the Sun against the sign of Pisces, and because of this gradual slippage backwards through the Zodiac we on Earth are now in the cusp, that is the junction, of Pisces and Aquarius, hence the 'Dawning of the Age of Aquarius'. (No one is certain of the exact date when the signs will change as each sign appears to occupy a different amount of the band of Zodiacal stars, called the ecliptic.) This means that if you rely on your horoscope in the papers and have always considered yourself to be an Aries, Taurus, Gemini or Cancer, etc., according to

21

Sidereal astrology you would actually be the previous sign; so Leos are really Cancer, and any Aries people will actually be Pisceans. When we get into Aquarius completely, we will reassess our Sun signs again.

Astrology is quite a complicated process because an individual horoscope is a unique diagram based on exactly when and where a person was born. Looking at the positions of the Sun and Moon and all the planets as seen from an individual's birthplace provides a pattern of stellar relationships that can indicate strengths or weaknesses, potential or difficulties in life. From the earliest time, sky-watchers have noticed that certain 'stars' seemed to move across the heavens; these wanderers are called the planets. Astrologers consider their positions in different Zodiac signs to construct a horoscope.

Sometimes individuals identify with an astrological sign, for example Leo or Capricorn, because that was the sign in the sky when they were born, with its special attributes. Similarly each of the Great Signs of the ages has a different characteristic. Without going into the art of astrology here, it is enough to recognize that the Age of Pisces was when people followed large scale movements in occupations, philosophy and religion – the early symbol used by the Christians was a fish. Aquarius is a Water Carrier who brings life-giving water to those in need, an individual helping others.

Paganism as an Alternative Way

In the last 2,000 years many mass movements have arisen, from the birth of the major book-based religions, to the development of cities, industry, the canals, the railways, the motor car, and more recently the telephone, television and computers. Most of these things, when they came into public awareness, were seen as beneficial. In hindsight, this has not always been the case. Factories employed a great many people, who had to quit rural activities to live crowded together in towns, striving within mines, iron works and workshops. Many of these industries brought pollution to the air, the rivers and the land. No one at the time realized the eventual consequences, which to a degree, afflict our world today. No one thought the Industrial Revolution would bring harm, but rather offer steady employment, stability and wealth. Cities grew, people were moved on railways and later by road, swarming like locusts across the land and dwelling in ever-increasing urban environments. Some of the country lore, skills and magics were lost at this time.

Through the ages Nature has been changed by humans, and humans have changed their relationship with Nature. Research in many fields of natural sciences, psychology and ecology has revealed all kinds of things about human nature, our innate skills and abilities in many fields of existence. While most of the material areas of life have been well catered for and explained, there are still things we don't understand and can't explain. Science talks of various space–time dimensions, whereas the esoteric world speaks of planes of existence. The realms our awareness enters in dream and visionary states may well be attempts at consciously entering other dimensions, time lines or states of being.

Understanding the Cosmos

The ancient Greeks defined matter as being divided into four elements: Earth, Water, Fire and Air. Now matter is thought to consist of particles, energies, waves and plasma. Things that are alive are animated by some as yet unexplained 'life force'. The cosmos came into being billions of years ago after an explosion from nothing into everything in potential. The Universe is continuing to expand at an increasing rate, stars are being born and dying fiery deaths as supernovas all the time. Major forces like gravity, electricity and magnetism are not fully understood, and the search for potential subatomic particles continues, with frequent discoveries, some of which defy logic or previously held theories. Particle physicists talk of strings of connectivity, of many dimensions bound with strings or meshes. M theory attempts to explain different string theories. The 'M' stands for mesh or membrane, but some consider it is magic. The mystery remains, yet science and magic continue as twin paths towards wisdom and understanding of the physical, mental, spiritual and esoteric worlds.

The Age of Aquarius might be different. Whereas the fishes of Pisces swam in schools together, the Aquarian Water Bearer carries a drinking vessel to share with others. It could become a time of helping other people rather than mass movements, an age of individuality and creativity, and a renewed sense of the sacred. The gradual change is allowing people to think for themselves, choose what they believe and how they want to discover and interact with what they consider to be sacred. To outsiders some of the 'New Age' ideas are rather strange.

Festivals to celebrate the passing seasons have always been part of our culture. Some are family gatherings, like Christmas, others are more personal for birthdays and anniversaries. Within smaller communities there have often been village dances, processions, well dressings, religious festivals and ancient local customs. These gatherings allowed many folk of the area to come together, to dress up, eat and drink, enact historical events or attend fetes and fairs. Such community activities, which still continue in many parts of the country, are very important, and getting involved in the planning and backstage aspects can be great fun.

Because people like to share spiritual or local activities, or find like-minded souls to celebrate with, a number of Pagan or neo-Pagan groups or impulses have become more widely known. Although it has often been thought that there has been a long-standing Pagan underworld functioning in Britain and Europe, that witch covens and magical lodges were meeting secretly for hundreds of years, this may not be the case. Certainly in the past each village would have had its wise folk, midwives, cunning men, blacksmiths, herbalists and healers. This is because organized medical treatment, doctors and hospitals, in the way that we recognize them today, are all products of the last couple of centuries. If you got ill, then you might consult the local herbwife, if your horse went lame you would take it to the farrier, or if you felt you had been ill-wished you would seek out witch or cunning man. All these people learned their skills from the world around them, valuing wild plants and inherited lore in problem-solving. As historians

24

tell us, there was no sense of these skilled folk being part of a Pagan faith or magical network.

Development of Pagan Ideas

The development of modern Pagan thought was influenced by a small number of writers from the 1950s onwards. At the end of the nineteenth century an interest in classical mythology with its heroes, Gods and Goddesses, archaeological discoveries, and secret societies like the Hermetic Order of the Golden Dawn became popularized, often through works of fiction. Other investigators were examining folk customs and traditional activities, morris dancing and folk tales for traces of an enduring Pagan current. Gradually these various sources of both fact and fiction awakened a real spiritual desire for the Old Religion, for local Gods and Goddesses, Mother Nature and the living spirits in trees and stones. The academics were trying to establish if there had been a Universal Mother Goddess and her cult back in antiquity. Others became interested in the ancient Gods of Egypt, or the heroes in Irish, Welsh and Scottish tradition. All these influenced the seekers of a new spirituality that combined reverence of Nature, ritual celebration and a continuing magical energy.

Today there are all kinds of Pagan currents, some individual like solo or hedgewitches, others in covens, groves or lodges. Some have a strict hierarchy being led by a Priestess, while others are looser groups, sharing traditional festivals throughout the year. Some of these people learn all they know from books, or family members, and others study courses or attend workshops. Anyone can profess to be a Pagan, and though some groups expect their followers to be initiated into their coven or lodge, many other people have discovered their own spiritual path. Most Pagans acknowledge one or many Goddesses and Gods, spirits of place, and the sacredness of Nature. Many accept the idea of reincarnation in that the human soul may live through different lifetimes, gaining experiences, knowledge and wisdom.

Followers of the Norse Gods are usually called Heathens and use rune symbols in their magic. Druids, Bards and Ovates follow

25

Celtic mythology, celebrate the seasons, some at Stonehenge and other ancient stone circles, and value learning, poetry and creativity. They use various forms of divination, some using images of native animals, practise alternative forms of healing and work with Nature and the seasons as closely as they can. Each of these Pagan practitioners will have a strong ethical background, giving help only when it is asked for and avoiding influencing the lives of others. Modern Pagan practice is a form of private spirituality. It is said that if you have five Pagans in a room you will have about seven different opinions!

Pagans have no set book of rules, no fixed hierarchy of priests or clergy, no buildings created by people for worship, no prescribed ceremonies of birth, marriage or death, or weekly meetings for communion, prayer or thanksgiving. Each person will develop their own pattern, often in conjunction with others, to mark the passing seasons, celebrate anniversaries and share forms of wedding, naming and memorial services. These are often held out of doors, in ancient earthworks, forests or stone monuments. Pagans feel that places blessed by the creative Spirits or Gods and Goddesses of their particular form of Paganism are equally holy. Many Pagans will meditate regularly, give thanks for good things and write prayers and poems for special occasions. Some prefer formalized rituals, creating a sacred space with the elements of Earth, Water, Fire and Air. Some may draw circles out of doors, or make a shrine or altar in their own homes. There is no set pattern, but what feels right. Nearly always aspects of Nature are taken into account: the phase of the Moon, the sign of the Zodiac, and the time of day, as all these add power to any spell.

2

EXPLORING WAYS OF HEALING FOR THE MIND, BODY AND SPIRIT

Witches and cunning men were often involved in arts of healing for both people and animals. In the days before modern medicine, with doctors and hospitals, each community would have a healer, a midwife and someone who helped deal with heartache and bad luck. These practitioners must have been known in their village, and from early written records, there seem to have been specialists for broken bones, for skin or eye complaints or illnesses in children. It is often thought that witches and magicians would have been illiterate in the past, as regular education didn't become widespread until the mid-1800s; however, these were people who valued knowledge. Because there are hundreds of plants, minerals, trees and herbs which have a part to play in potion- and spell-making, the wise ones would have sought out any new sources of information they could. Records exist to show that because actual shops as we know them were rare outside big cities, there was a sort of mail order system where books could be dispatched from publishers to their customers. New books on medicine, herbs or even magical arts, often translated into English from Greek, Latin or later Arabic would be of interest and possibly passed around and copied by those who valued them.

Witches and herbwives would have inherited knowledge from their parents and other older folk in their community. This would provide them with an accurate map of the sources of certain herbs throughout the year. Everyone walked about far more than we do today, so the woods and hedgerows acted in the way shops do now. If a witch or wizard needed a particular plant, its location would be clear in their memories. Every healer would preserve plant material by drying it, or making it into potions or pills using oils, vinegar, honey and beeswax. Knowing which herbs were available at any time of the year was an important aspect of their knowledge. Traditionally herbalists recognized what we would consider to be the chemical constituents of any material, but also its 'virtue'. Virtue is the invisible, magical aspect of anything, which changes it from an ordinary stick or stone or leaf or other substance in the healer's collection to a curative substance. Many things have virtue by where they grow, perhaps on a traditional sacred site or near a healing spring, or have virtue added by the healer's art, to make them effective.

Not only would the place certain things came from be significant, but the phase of the Moon, or the season of the year would be taken into account. Healing potions were, and are, thought to be influenced as to whether the Moon is waxing or waning. Gathering herbs at sunrise gives them different qualities to picking them in the evening. The old witches and healers gradually learned about these subtle influences during their lifetimes, and although today we can quickly look up which herb might ease which condition, little is written about where and when that plant should be gathered, how it should be prepared and when it will be most effective. The same goes for using tree leaves, bark or twigs which are often made into teas or tinctures.

Stones too have a place in the equipment of a working healer, though not necessarily shiny or pretty crystals, shattered from their rocky bed to be sold at high prices. Any common pebble can be magicked into a curative charm if the right knowledge and ritual is applied to it. Gaining the insight to sense the subtle energies and virtue of anything and to know if it will work its magic effectively is all part of a lengthy training process. This cannot safely be hurried.

Everyone May be Able to Heal

Everyone has some healing ability, whether being a calm voice in a family crisis, or applying a direct skill such as massage, or making a herbal tea. In any case, it is important to discover the root of the ailment, and if you want to use healing it is worth joining a real course of instruction and then practising on yourself. Consider the idea of health. This Anglo-Saxon word comes from the same source as the word for wholeness. Healing is making whole. But what does that wholeness consist of? We are all aware of our physical bodies, any long-term conditions, any damage we have sustained, and any sense of discomfort. These are all aspects of our physical selves which are affected by how we live, what we eat, how stressed we are, even whether we get enough rest and sleep. All these are things which we can alter, and for which we each have a responsibility. One of the first concepts of healing of any sort is to establish our own underlying state of health, not only in body but in mind and spirit too. This is one part of the ancient motto 'Know Thyself', which was written on an ancient Greek temple. It is a key concept of practical magic. Being outdoors puts you in touch with the *Natural* Health Service!

You need to explore your own self, being completely honest and open. This can be a secret process, but it often helps to write down what you feel about your body in a diary. Such journals are kept by witches and magicians to record dreams, the results of meditations, the process of any spell or charm or ritual, and its outcome. These books are often referred to as 'magical diaries' and they should be entirely private and ideally written by hand on paper! It is the first magical act for any trainee witch or wizard to obtain a nice hardback book which can be used in this way. A book is quick to refer back to, to add odd jottings and inspiration and quotes from something you have read or been told. This record is easily portable, cannot be hacked or duplicated and is an important tool in your voyage of self-discovery. The four precepts of magical art are 'To Know, to Will, to Dare and to Keep Silent'.

The Four Powers of the Natural Magician

To Know
Knowledge will come as you progress upon your path, both from study and experience. As you get to understand yourself and explore Nature, this will give you the tools to work the magic of change. Knowledge is essential, ideally based on experience rather than the internet. Never undervalue reading books or talking to people. None is wasted.

To Will
The concept of Will is what empowers any spell or magical work. It is not greed nor desire for something, but a deep understanding of what ought to be done. True Will directs a practitioner towards a specific goal. Learning your true Will takes time and openness of heart because you will need to explore your motives for anything you want to do. It gives you willpower.

To Dare
Daring is another seemingly old-fashioned concept, yet because it is tied in with soul-searching honesty before taking action, it can be very hard. If you are seriously wanting to explore spiritual matters, and discover how they can be applied to Nature and human nature, this will take daring. Every act of true magic is an experiment so the outcome isn't always what was expected. It is not about taking on dangerous activities or performing feats of strength, but of having the courage to seek answers to life's hard questions. These include 'Who am I?', 'What is my purpose here on Earth?' and sometimes 'Can you help me?'. These are all aspects of the great question of knowing yourself, and usually the one with the answers is yourself.

The Importance of Silence

Keeping silent can be a real challenge into today's world of instant messaging, immediate communications and ongoing interfaces. Much magical skill comes from individual action, deeply personal feelings and honest insight. You will be building up a new relationship with the natural world, energies and perhaps unseen beings of various kinds. Moving silently and keeping your mouth shut will allow you to get closer to Nature. As you venture into the spiritual realms, you may encounter all kinds of wonders, have strange and unsettling experiences and make new discoveries about yourself and the world around you. Obviously you might want to share some of this knowledge, but if you do talk freely about it some of this hidden work can lose its power. Like water from a leaking bottle, it will spread around and be lost.

Silence is also a quality which aids meditation, brings inner calm, and allows the deeper levels of your being to be perceived. Finding a silent place may take you away from your everyday environment, yet if you are able to access a natural place, a garden, a wood or a river bank, you will find a different quality of life. Sitting under a tree and just letting human sound ebb away will open up your subtle sense of hearing, which is useful in magic.

The other side of silence is actually listening. When someone asks you for help it is essential that you really pay attention to what they say, and how they are saying it. If you wish to practise some healing art, it is important to get proper training and guided experience. Most alternative forms of treatment, similar to those used by the wise folk of old, can't be learned from a book or a weekend course. All forms of healing require an understanding of the life force, of what makes people ill, and how much they want to share in the process of getting better. Some people believe that it is the doctor or prescription which will make them well, a treatment applied by someone else rather than a co-operative relationship between the patient, their illness and the healer/doctor or treatment. If the patient, whether being cared for with orthodox medicine or anything else, won't listen to advice, take the pills at the proper time or in the right way, they will not benefit. Most kinds of esoteric healing first require the patient to be honest, to have received a proper diagnosis from a qualified person and to have recognized they have to join in the healing process. Healing won't be done for them or to them by any kind of healer without them being a participant.

What is Health?

Illness and wholeness involve body, mind and spirit. If your body is sick this will also impact upon your mind, because you don't feel well. The more you worry about your condition, the worse you might feel. If you don't have the mental courage to find out what is actually the problem, then that adds to the concern that it might be worse than you think. For this reason it is important to discover what the problem is. Information will certainly help your mind to deal with your condition and begin to find strategies to aid healing. The more you fret, the greater delay in setting out a plan for returning to health. Often a simple, mental statement 'I will get better' goes a long way to starting this process. Things like pain and lack of sleep will not allow the natural healing energies to work with whatever treatment you are using. If you are able to mentally take yourself to a place of peace and relaxation this will be in your favour. Ideally if you are able to actually go to a natural, outdoor space this can be curative.

Recent research has shown that woodland gives off chemicals that can be beneficial to people. Even looking at pictures of trees for fifteen minutes can lower blood pressure, as will stroking a pet. Modern hospitals often have huge photographs of landscapes or forests to help calm patients, even having prints of branches and leaves on the ceiling of corridors leading to operating theatres. Waiting areas now seem to have pictures of flowers or fruiting trees on their walls.

Because ill-health affects the body, which usually needs to be treated with physical therapies, little attention is given to the spiritual or soul dimension. In the past healers would consider this hidden aspect of someone asking for help. The terms 'dispirited' or 'soul-sick' imply that some problems are deep-seated. Feeling discomfort at a spiritual level can definitely hamper a body's natural desire for balance and wholeness, so finding things or places which are uplifting or increase happiness are steps in the right direction.

This is where another traditional magical skill can come into play, which is 'Creative Visualization'. To be able to imagine, remember or invent a scene so vividly it seems real, using concentration and willpower is what gives many magical processes their effectiveness. Because magic is about causing change, being able to picture a changed or healed situation is a way to make it real. If you consider the images you get in dreams, they are made up of memories, but often of scenes, events or people doing things they haven't done in your waking life. It is possible to dream of places you haven't visited. It is similar images that you have to mentally envision in creative visualization. Regularly remembering your dreams is another valuable magical practice, and another series of things to enter into your magical diary.

The Origins of Magic and Sacred Objects

From earliest times humans thought every object had a spirit or God dwelling within, whether it was a tree, a spring, a rock, the sea, the wind or an animal. People interacted with these powers by verbal supplication, by threats or by offerings. Rhythmic sounds affect deep parts of the brain, so possibly the first 'prayers' were repeated words or mantras. Now a chant or verse is known as a spell to attract the attention of a power to act favourably towards the spell-weaver.

The first magical objects were probably stones with holes through them, or fossils, or strange shaped natural objects. Children still collect these as magical items. The holey or holy stone held an ice crystal and was a lens with which to make fire. Stone Age arrowheads or fossil belemnites were thought to be shot by faery folk, to bring disease. Spiral ammonites or 'petrified snakes', have been worn as lucky charms for hundreds of years.

Often amulets of stone or clay were shaped like an eye. These watched for danger so were protective. This 'eye motif' has continued to be used, worn as a charm, painted on the prows of boats, or hung around the necks of children, for protection. These items don't contain their own luck, but they attract benefit to their wearers, perhaps being thought to be the 'All-Seeing Eye' of a deity. Something long ago must have started this magical awareness. Objects hold power, words can attract the attention of invisible, helpful beings. These beliefs continue to this day.

Magicians learned how to shape these forces so that their spells were effective. The results are more than a 'placebo' effect. Now more sophisticated lucky charms are made from precious stones, or bone, or even plastic. Superstitious people in sports or the theatre continue to rely on them. The old magics still have power.

Good Luck or Bad Luck

Many of the items used as lucky charms or mascots have been considered to have beneficial or protective qualities. Some things are lucky in one country but seen as ill omens in another. For example, in Britain black cats are lucky, but in America and other parts of the world a white cat brings luck and black ones bode ill. Breaking a mirror was thought to mean seven years ill luck because these mysterious reflecting glasses were so rare and expensive they cost years of wages to replace, also the images captured might be harmed by the shattering glass. Walking under a ladder might mean you get paint spattered on you, but in the past breaking the Holy Trinity outlined by the triangle they formed meant you could anger God. There are hundreds of such ideas preserved in folklore and custom. Finding a four-leaf clover was fortunate, as it represented the trinity of faith, hope and charity, yet had an extra dimension of luck. 'One leaf for fame, one for wealth, one for a true lover, and one for eternal health.'

Aspects of Ancient Magic

The first writing on a magical subject was in cuneiform. This wedge-shaped writing system developed in Mesopotamia (now Iraq) about 6,000 years ago. It showed the positions of the stars and the planets, which were important in astronomy and astrology.

Writing conveyed messages between strangers, recorded events and described places at a distance. Early inscriptions showed the positions of stars and planets, marked boundaries and recorded rules. Maybe the marks around cave paintings were the first alphabets. Unfortunately records on wood have mostly been destroyed by time. Egyptian hieroglyphs written on papyrus or carved on stone told of Gods and Goddesses, prayers and protective spells. Records show a God of magic called Heka who was invoked for aid; Isis was the Great Mother; Thoth, the Lord of Wisdom and the Moon; and Sheshet, the Lady of Books. There are ancient texts on medicine, restoring life to mummies and charms to be worn for protection.

The Greeks overran Egypt and brought Goddesses of wisdom and magic. The three-faced Hekate, related to Heka, ruled the underworld and magical arts. Dreams, sleep, death and fate all had their own deities. People consulted entranced Oracular Priestesses at Delphi where mysterious prophesies were made. Aesclepius, God of healing, had temples where patients' dreams were analyzed to find cures.

His symbolic staff, entwined with a snake, is still used to show a pharmacy or clinic. Later the Romans left Latin inscriptions on stone, metal, wax and wood which can still be read. They had forms of divination using omens of flights of birds, and geomancy, when marks made on the ground were interpreted according to sixteen figures. They also wore fertility amulets in the shape of a phallus of stone or clay. Archaeologists have found lamps, ornaments and carved fertility bringers. Lucky phalluses made of coral are still worn widely today.

As the centuries passed different approaches to magical and divinatory arts were established with varying results. In the countryside the village witches, cunning men and herbalists still had their place and were consulted for advice, medicines and foretelling the future. These were important and valued skills in village life. However, the healers who seemed to hold the keys to life and death were held in awe in their communities, or even feared. The Medieval church rejected older arts and protective spells. Divination, conjuring spirits, blood offerings or curses, and even healing were banned. The old arts went underground so that folk healers, village witches and wizards practised their skills in secret. Alchemists, who tried chemical experiments to make gold and useful drugs, worked in hidden laboratories. Grimoires, the textbooks of magical techniques are still to be found in libraries, and herbal knowledge, astrology, Tarot divination, magic and spell-weaving are still widely practised by all sorts of people today.

Value of Myths and Legends

Much magical wisdom has been hidden in myths and legends. People recognize the names of wizards like Merlin or Gandalf. The stories kept old knowledge alive and are now sci-fi epics, modern novels or films, but the occult essence can still be recognized. Poetry from the Middle Ages can call up powerful emotions, music can charm, old objects in museums retain their magical charge, and will bespell those open to their influences. Mathematics was a secret science and numerology was a way of finding meaning in numbers, names and dates. Scrying or crystal gazing was another way to learn about the future or matters at a distance. Dr John Dee developed a magical language, carved wax talismans of protection and talked to angels. His astrological knowledge brought success to Elizabeth I's reign when he chose her coronation date.

Signs of Good or Evil

The Romans had several forms of omen divination based on birds. An odd number of birds flying from the left was thought lucky, for example. If the sacred geese kept at the Temple of Jupiter in ancient Rome ate grain from the right side of their food, it could mean war and if from the left, it would tell of the success or death of emperors.

Clouds, patterns of tea leaves or coffee grounds, twigs, shapes of stones, car numbers and almost anything which appears suddenly can be seen as an omen. People still choose lucky numbers for lotteries, or notice signs in froth on coffee, shapes of tree branches or strange clouds and judge these as good or bad omens. Colours, names and even TV adverts can be imbued with mystical import for good or ill. Often the ancients had seers who would have dreams or enter oracular trances and see shapes in smoke. These signs would be interpreted by the Priests as positive or negative omens.

To dream of pigs was lucky in many places. Today pigs made of marzipan are eaten for luck at Christmas, and in China, because sows have lots of piglets, they are symbols of fertility and plenty. Seeing a hare in a field was fortunate, and it is really the hare that turned into the Easter Bunny, a symbol of approaching Spring. However, rabbits were ill omens if seen by fishermen on the way to their boats, and were thought to indicate a poor catch and a rough sea.

Animals and Magic

Many ordinary animals have a magical life. Cats kept as pets were thought to be familiar spirits that witches could send out to gather information or cause harm. Bats and their nocturnal flight were feared and hedgehogs were supposed to drink milk from cows lying down in fields. People used to have dried rabbits feet as lucky charms, or pieces of orange coral worn for protection. Toads were seen as uncanny, and a toad's bone prepared in a magical way was used to bespell horses. Images of dragons and unicorns were seen as power symbols in many cultures, and these mythical creatures are often found on the coats of arms of cities.

The ancient Egyptians had humanlike Gods with animal or bird heads; Hathor was the cow-headed Goddess of motherhood, Bast the cat was protective, and the jackal Anubis was the doglike guardian and guide. The dung beetle scarab, symbol of the undying Sun, is still used as a charm made of clay or gemstone to this day. Thoth, the God of wisdom, was associated with the ibis bird and also with baboons.

Tribes all over the world sought protection from their totem animal, especially bears, lions, wolves and jaguars.

In the Middle Ages keeping a pet was uncommon. Dogs were used for herding sheep and guarding cattle, and ladies living in cold castles kept lap dogs as living hotwater bottles, but cats or birds were seldom kept as pets. Horses were protected by magic with iron shoes and brasses decorated with Pagan symbols, or holy stones hung over their stables.

It has always been acknowledged that animals have extra senses, dogs know when their owner is coming home, birds react before earthquakes, and cats watch invisible things move around their homes.

Traditional horsemen and women adopt body postures shown by other horses to befriend or challenge unbroken animals. They act as surrogate parents or herd leaders to wayward foals and teach them to behave. This sort of knowledge, brought about by long-term observation of the horses or other wild animals, has been used to interact with them for thousands of years. Often grooms would sing or whistle as they worked with their plough teams, to encourage them and reassure them. Some charmers develop special potions of herbs which affect the animals, in the same way that cats are enchanted by catnip toys. If you know what smells scare animals or attract them to you, you can appear to have control. Magical horse whisperers used to prepare a toad bone by steeping it in magical mixture, which could cause a fierce stallion to stop in its tracks, or a tired horse go on.

The influence of superstition is less strong these days but people still keep up these ancient practices. Crossing your fingers for luck, when a lottery is drawn, is another superstition that goes back to early Christian times. However, 'touch wood' is far older, calling upon the God Pan to look after you. Rings are important symbols as they are endless, and wedding rings are worn on the third finger of the left hand, thought by ancient people, to link directly to the heart. This was recorded by Galen, a Greek physician, in the first century AD. Gold is the metal of the Sun and does not tarnish.

Tokens of Luck or Protection

From prehistoric times it seems that our ancestors experienced special qualities of certain objects, perhaps a fossil or a strange shaped stone, an eye formed on the branch of a tree which they felt brought them luck or averted harm. Gradually these items became more elaborate or formal, developing into what are usually called amulets. Specifically for protection, these are usually flat discs of metal, wood or bone, which have mysterious diagrams or symbols on them. Most are again passive, that is once set up, they don't need anything to keep working, but are specifically protective. Some of the oldest seem to be painted eye shapes, now often made of blue glass, which invoke the power of an all-seeing God to protect the person, boat or house on which they are found. Some are actually carefully prepared sigils or magical images carved by a magician of great power. These are designed to control unseen entities, or protect from evil during the working of deep magic.

At the time of Elizabeth I Dr John Dee found a way to talk to angelic spirits, with the help of a scryer or crystal gazer who needed to be guarded by elaborate amulets made of wax, as in a trance he sought information from invisible beings. These magical discs have survived and some are in the British Museum. To Catholics medals depicting saints are amulets, as are the Hebrew or Arabic texts inscribed on precious metal, worn or fixed to doorposts. The Key of Solomon contains many diagrams made up of words in ancient languages, symbols of planets or magical signs called sigils. These can be copied on to metal or card to make various protective amulets.

3

MAGIC IS THE ART OF CAUSING, RECOGNIZING AND SHAPING CHANGE

As the three strands of knowledge that form the basis of spiritual ecology are each so vast it is necessary to look at some of the history of magic, sometimes called the 'science of the soul', the way humanity has interacted with Nature in its broadest form; and aspects of our inner or spiritual worlds. Since the beginning of time people have collected or created objects which have strange or beneficial properties. Archaeologists describe these ancient items as charms or amulets, for magic or healing, luck bringers or talismans to ward off harm. We still have 'lucky charms' on key rings or mobile phones. Even Neanderthals decorated shells with ochre to wear. In caves they painted amazing images of animals and birds, believed to be hunting magic, or to honour their prey. These 40,000-year-old images use the shape of the rock to show animals in 3D.

Demanding help from the unseen through the secret arts of talisman-making still exists. Football teams have animal mascots, and fans have spell-like chants to encourage their chosen team. Historic places sell souvenirs of Cornish Piskies, Holy Water and copies of magical objects. All over the world, strange 'cult objects', spells written in hieroglyphs, phallic carvings or holey stones are displayed. Some are requests to the Gods for justice or for assistance. Ancient magic arts still practised, not because we are superstitious and gullible, but because we know they work from hundreds of years of experience.

Some people had abilities for finding food, fresh water or shelter for their tribe long before villages were established. These survival skills are real magic. If the sorcerer's divinations failed the tribe could starve. Today we don't need to rely on the wild for sustenance, but people still read their horoscopes. People have lucky numbers or colours, or horseshoes or prayers on a wall, or we cross our fingers for luck, or throw spilled salt over the left shoulder to ward off harm. The old superstitions are an unconscious belief in magic.

Different Sorts of Magical Working

From ancient times there have been magic workers in most communities. Sometimes these people were honoured and respected, seen as Priests or Priestesses of the local deities, and consulted when help was needed. At other times in history the magic workers were scorned or feared or outlawed. The names they were referred by, including witch or warlock, were insults and could lead to accusations, trials and sometimes death. The roots of the word 'witch' are obscure, although many consider it to be related to 'wise'; it could also mean crooked in the way that withies are bent to weave baskets, valuable containers for herbs, food or perhaps knowledge. 'Wicca' is a term now used to define those who become members of a coven, or in some places as a general self-description. It seems to have been first written as 'Wica' by Gerald Gardner, whose book *High Magic's Aid* began to popularize this Pagan philosophy or religion. Wicca was originally pronounced 'witcha'. Warlock seems to derive from Anglo-Saxon *waerloga*, which meant 'lie teller' or deceiver. It isn't really the proper name for a male witch. Wizard does appear to have connections with the concept of wisdom, as these were people who sought knowledge in a more controlled and book-learned way. Today you can be a male witch or a female wizard, if you really want a label, although some people are still wary of people who call themselves witches.

Magic workers have also been involved in High or Ceremonial Magic. This is a formal system, often based on ancient knowledge from Egypt, the Middle East or Greece, for example. As these civilizations were literate, written accounts of their esoteric arts and mystical skills have been preserved, at least in part. Formal schools of magic, secret societies and lodges were developed to explore and make use of ritual forms, symbols, arcane alphabets and elaborate robes and equipment, which assisted with the focus and intent in High Magic. Some such schools continue to this day, although they do not usually advertise their existence nor canvass for students. Real magical training takes years because it is a vast field of knowledge which can be dangerous in the hands of the untrained. The simpler arts of the folk magicians, country witches or cunning men rely far more on the natural materials in the countryside, and the powers of Earth, Water, Fire, Air and the Spirit of Creation.

Village witches would be well aware of the phases of the Moon, the locations of healing plants, sacred springs of water, and where and when the veil between the realms of the seen and the unknown were thin. Often this knowledge was built up over generations when families lived in the same area for many hundreds of years. Although the Industrial Revolution shifted many people from the countryside to towns and cities, the old ways were preserved in rural areas, although political, religious and social movements eroded patterns of celebration.

Conjurors were originally people who could raise spirits or apparitions, but this term is used now to suggest an entertainer who uses tricks to delight or mystify an audience. Sometimes these showmen are referred to as Stage Magicians, demonstrating card tricks and sleight of hand. Very few of them believe that magic is a real force, and what they do is for the amusement or bafflement of spectators. Some of them have made quite a lot of money misleading or cheating those who watch the show. Real magic seldom enriches the witch, wizard or magical worker, whose aim is to gain wisdom in order to help or heal. Doing this well can be reward enough.

Druids, Shamans and Witches

Other terms used in esoteric literature include shaman or druid. Each of these is a particular strand of knowledge. Originally shamans came from tribal areas in Siberia and the far north, where the population moved with their animals from season to season. Shamans were and are healers who work with the world of human spirit as well as Nature, using drumming, chanting or plant extracts to enter trances when they can explore otherworldly realms. Sometimes they would offer potions, and ritual dances around a sick person so that they could be made whole. Often the shaman had been very ill and could only be cured by taking on the role as tribal healer too. People who have not had a 'near death experience' yet proclaim themselves to be shamans are not following the traditional path.

Druids are recorded by the Romans as a priesthood of the Celtic people in Europe, leading ceremonies, offering sacrifices of animals, but sometimes valuable metal swords or shields cast into rivers, which were believed to be entrances to the Otherworld where their Gods dwelt. They were able to divine the future, bring about healing, act as law-givers, teachers and judges, and retain the memory of their people in verse and song. They would chant spells to ward off enemies in times of war, and were so feared by the Roman invaders that great efforts were made to put them to death. Because Druids did not write down their lore but relied on the power of the human memory, or of place, or of sensitivity of trained diviners, much of their natural wisdom has been lost. Their Bardic skill was to remember lore through poetry and storytelling They held their meetings in groves of trees and developed a special relationship with wild places from which they drew wisdom, collected medicinal and magical plants and read oracles in the flights of birds and shapes of clouds.

Today there are many followers of Druidry, belonging to one of the teaching organizations like the Order of Bards, Ovates and Druids, or one of the groups based at Glastonbury and elsewhere. Some of these modern Druids hold public ceremonies to celebrate the Solstices and Equinoxes and other traditional feast days or annual gatherings. Each individual follows their own path of learning, creative arts and healing skills under the guidance of a mentor, but can come together in Groves for instruction or ritual. For divination purposes they may use twigs of special trees, engraved with Ogham letters or may use modern Oracle Cards depicting native trees or wild animals, and express themselves through storytelling and verse, seeking spiritual gifts from Mother Earth.

Although today there is a wide variety of magical practitioners, witches, wizards, druids, shamans and other cunning folk, traditionally these people worked in conjunction with guiding Gods or spirits. Some of these inspiring entities were or are real people, some are folk heroes, some local deities, spirits of holy springs or faery folk. Some may be Christian saints, or Goddesses named by the Romans, the Anglo-Saxons or the Celts, although accurate written records are rare. Often they are linked to a specific place, and one of the tasks of a modern seeker of spiritual inspiration and wisdom is to find out who, in their area, might help. Learning about history, both local and worldwide, provides roots for many aspects of human spiritual growth. History also teaches us how and where people have succeeded and where their activities have failed or caused harm to Nature.

Echoes of Sacred Places and People

Place names, especially those of old villages, now embedded in towns and cities, may hold echoes of some sacred being or some holy well. Old maps can be very helpful if you want to find your local Goddess, or where faery folk used to be seen. Most county libraries hold actual copies of maps, old land charters and ownership directories. These old books give a wonderful insight into who built your house and who has lived there over time. Other documents show ancient water courses, wells and springs. It is written that 'a city may move, but not a well'. Many ancient springs were dedicated to a particular saint or other holy being, and often they were associated with a particular sort of healing. St Ives in Cornwall has a well whose water traditionally helped with eye conditions.

Places associated with folk heroes are known all over the land, like Robin Hood in Sherwood Forest or King Arthur in Avalon.

There may well have been an actual Robin who lived in the green-wood, or a King of post-Roman Britain about whom the Arthurian legends are told. In these and many other tales there is a mystery concealed within a long remembered story. According to the story, Robin Hood lived in a forest and took riches from travellers to give to the poor folk. King Arthur and his band of knights were guided by the wizard Merlin and after all sorts of challenges, quested for the Holy Grail through ancient forests. No one is exactly certain what it is or where it might be found, but it echoes the magical cauldrons of Celtic Legends. The Holy Grail has been described as a chalice or a stone or another miraculous object, and the finding of this will heal the Wasteland.

The Wasteland

The 'Wasteland' could have been a region destroyed by war, by drought, flood or famine. Some evidence has been found in patterns of narrow tree rings that suggest lack of sunshine for several years, possibly caused by volcanic ash in the atmosphere. When the land was laid waste something had to be found to heal it; perhaps this healing just occurred naturally with time.

However, now our world is becoming a new Wasteland with increasing forest fires, floods, landslides and droughts. The whole world has woken up to the fact that climate change is real and that urgent action is necessary. It is predicted both by scientists and seers that the Earth is reaching a critical turning point and unless swift and decisive action is taken by every nation disaster will follow. This may seem an enormous challenge, especially for individuals, but those who have any awareness, or any care for the planet we live on, will be prepared to do what they can. Certainly many matters can be dealt with, like using less of everything, including energy, clothes, food which must not be wasted, and other consumables. It won't be enough to halt global warming on its own, but it will be a step in the right direction. If everyone encouraged all those around them also to take action, recycle, share, exchange or make do and mend, rather than always buying new stuff it could make a huge difference.

45

Those who understand magical arts can add that into the healing process too.

Looking for Spiritual Guidance

Ancient myths of Gods and Goddesses, legends of heroes and folk tales retain aspects of ancient wisdom, and with careful personal meditation can help today's practitioners discover their own Earth healing powers. In many places there were local heroes, hermits, rulers, saints and wise folk who sought and taught aspects of local lore and offered healing or divination to those who asked. In spirit they are still there today. There are many useful sources of information about the magic and spiritual forces to be found almost everywhere. Just as everyone has the potential to learn and use magic, most locations have a deep spiritual foundation underlying the modern world. Anyone on a quest to connect with the spirit of Nature, even if in a large city, will find magical and mystical areas, often in the most surprising places. Don't forget, though smothered with human construction, underneath it all Mother Earth endures, her sacred waters still flow, and the powerful rays of Sun and Moon and Stars shine down. By opening your eyes through meditation and magical visualization these forces can become clear and potent aspects of Nature. They can bring enlightenment, energy and esoteric power once you know how to use them.

Discovering which Gods or Goddesses touch your heart is part of the path of your own spiritual awakening. Often by using book study and actual exploration of any natural places you will be drawn to particular deities, or sacred guides who can aid your journey. The quest for a spiritual direction has to become a personal pilgrimage to known sacred places, or to some forgotten wood, beach, spinney or garden. There is no concept of 'you must believe this', nor a creed to recite, nor a book to follow. The path is individual, and when you start to seek information, especially if you meditate on what you discover, often a clear vision shows itself to you. It must be meaningful and positive, helpful and life-enhancing, so that you know what is true for you. Finding a new power to worship, or festivals to celebrate are important and so is becoming aware of a personal connection with both the Earth as a planet, and as a spiritual being in her own right.

Over time humans have developed all sorts of relationships with the Gods and Goddesses, the spirits and the ethereal beings which inhabit the wild places. Some of these have been feared and offerings and sacrifices have been made to assuage any negative feelings. Others have been seen as Mother or Father figures, showing benign care to their earthly children. Many of the elves, faery folk and elemental spirits have had a less friendly relationship with people, who after all, have cut down their sacred woods, ploughed the wild flower meadows, destroyed their habitat and that of their familiar wild creatures to build roads and houses. They don't have a lot to thank us for, so it is no wonder that they have been thought of as malign or spiteful. It isn't too late, however, as people today are tentatively rebuilding their trust, honouring their sacred groves, or holy wells.

It is possible to see some of the Fair Folk if you sit very quietly at twilight in a natural place. Be absolutely still and silent, focus on a tree or plant, watch how the wind moves the leaves, and allow your mind to drift. After a while, if you mentally send out friendly invitations to whoever is around, you may begin to see a shadow or a shape in the greenery if your request is answered. They may take all kinds of forms, from flickers of light in a rain drop, to a face half hidden in the leaves. You have no right to command them, but if you have an honest intention to connect you may well be rewarded. Be patient and it will work for you.

Otherworldly Beings

Throughout history, the Faery folk, the Fae, Elves, Sprites, Goblins and Leprechauns have lived in the shadows. Some have been helpful, such as Brownies who did housework at night, or faeries who caused butter to form in the churn, or protected livestock. Folk tales have been told all over the world of people's relationship with otherworldly beings. Some were seen as animals, Black Dogs or White Hinds, or as 'mythical creatures' like Unicorns or Mermaids, Dragons or Elementals. Each of these, and many more, are real in their own realms, just as magic is real in ours. We may not believe in magic, nor have the skill to use it, nor to be able to see the Fae, but we are able to learn these arts, if we accept that worlds of reality and dream overlap. This task is not easy, and it is not quick as we have had centuries of time to forget the old alliances, the mystical skills, the divining arts, and the healing charms that used to be parts of the human experience.

Magic relies on experience of the unseen, acknowledging the power of angels, spirits and elementals, which are thought to live partly in this world and partly in another dimension which we enter in dreams and visions. Faeries, angels and spirits of the place can be called upon for advice, healing or guidance. They may be part of 'Dark Matter', the unknown substance which makes up a large part of the cosmos, or the Mother Goddess, the Dark Mater. They may appear, or be called to us on occasions. Some magicians perform rituals to open links with these realms, using incense, incantation, a magical circle of protection and a very clear purpose. Nature spirits can be seen by sitting still in a wood, allowing the faces to appear in trees or among grasses. You could offer flowers, milk, honey or wine to accompany your request. Be patient; these elemental beings are nervous and dance to a slower music of life.

Ghosts may be encountered in many historical places. They have been photographed in doorways, on staircases and above the ground, because they exist between the worlds. Many ghosts are in modern dress and so pass by us unnoticed, or vanish when we try to look directly at them. Even CCTV cameras at stately homes have recorded them occasionally. Some people sense presences rather than seeing figures, or notice cold areas in buildings. Becoming aware of invisible beings or atmospheres shows your subtle, magical senses are growing, and is a valuable step in your spiritual life. By opening up your subtle senses through meditation, quietness and dream recall, it can be possible to discover or relearn many of these ancient abilities. Often students of magic or witchcraft find that when something is shown to them, or taught, like dowsing, it is familiar, almost as if they knew it before.

Angels are messengers of God and can be called upon for help, healing, comfort and advice. Many old magical arts are devoted to talking to angelic beings. Some are seen at moments of crisis, while others are deliberately called upon for guidance or protection.

Mother Nature

One of the most widely held ideas concerns Mother Nature. Many ancient religions honour, worship and offer thanksgiving prayers to the Great Goddess. She has many names, such as Gaia or the Earth Mother, as well as more personal titles like Isis, Ceres or Aphrodite. In the past everyone recognized the fact that they had a mother, even if their father's identity was not so certain. The Great Goddess was thought of as the actual planet Earth, and was recognized as a nourisher and nurturer of people. She was asked for help, particularly in regard of growing plants, and of caring for children. She was thanked at seasonal festivals with gifts of the first fruits, or for providing clean water, healing springs, and all the trees which provide wood. In some places Priestesses became her mouthpiece,

49

offering oracular speech in caves or sacred groves. Much of her worship seems to have involved song, dance, processions and sharing of harvests. Like many Pagan celebrations, these were acts of joy, fertility and celebration.

Coming to recognize a female deity for yourself, often in triple form, could be quite a leap of faith, but no one is forced to believe anything or accept religious concepts from outside on the paths of spiritual ecology. What can be considered, however, is that there are three aspects of creation as we know it. The first is space, the Universe, the heavens seen by some as the starry firmament, giving birth explosively to all matter, including the star-stuff within us all. The second mother is the Great Ocean, which gave birth to all life forms, evolving from the simplest single cell creatures to all the plants, animals, fish, birds and, later, people. Our third mother is that of the planet Earth, our home and sustainer. We are fed by things that grow on the planet, housed in materials derived from Earth, lit by the Sun and Moon, which shine upon us, bringing day and night and the seasons of the year. Every material thing we possess has originally come from Earth, maybe shaped by us, and after our death our remains will surely be returned to the earth. Our human history is written with ancient stone monuments, the use of precious metals in our personal devices and all the things that humans have created over a million years.

Many religions have records of virgin or unwed Goddesses giving birth to hero or a divine child, whose life forms the basis of sacred text or patterns of celebration and worship. Some of these holy beings have actually lived on Earth, while others are recorded in myth and folk memory. Each is important, as the lessons they taught or the ethics they lived by are relevant today. The holy books from the past are worth reading, not to be accepted wholesale, but individually considered for their inherent wisdom and guidance. Meditation on religious texts is always rewarding, as many of these divine teachers were healers or passed on knowledge from sacred sources, angels or deities. Many of the sites associated with them still hold power, for magic is frequently part of these ancient traditions.

Often the priesthood later lost its magic, didn't understand the real messages from its founders, and so feared anyone who used magic, healing or divination. This led to persecutions and condemnation. Much beneficial magic was suppressed.

Aspects of God

Pagans often have male Gods associated with the Sun, like Horus or Ra of the ancient Egyptians, or Helios or Apollo of the Greeks. They also venerate various Gods of Nature, like Pan or Faunus. Sometimes these Gods are nameless, like the many foliate faces or 'Green Men' found in old churches and public buildings. This living symbol of the resurgence of Nature, Spring after Winter, has never been fully explained. Gods die, either sacrificed or overthrown, while the Goddess changes but never dies.

Orthodox faiths have single male Gods, too. Some of these have a female partner, often later written out of scriptures by a male priesthood, but all divine beings had mothers as well as holy fathers. The Catholic Church compensated for a lack of actual Goddesses by upgrading holy women such as Mary, mother of Jesus, and accepted female saints as mediators between God, the priesthood and the congregation. Such holy ladies could be petitioned for protection, to bring spiritual gifts and for consolation. There are shrines in caves or grottos where such mystical women have appeared, and their sacred powers acknowledged. Many of the springs or caverns or rounded hill tops associated with Christian saints were thought of as sacred long before the time of Jesus, as archaeological finds at such shrines prove. It is sometimes possible to follow the evolution from some ancient deity of a healing well as her name gets changed to that of a saint. This is a whole area of spiritual research.

4

TRANSFORMATION THROUGH CHANGE

Humans have always changed things around them. Archaeological discoveries have shown that people found ways of shaping wood over 40,000 years ago. Gradually they learned to knap flint into sharp blades of various shapes and applications. They must have used wood and other plant material, stones and sticks to make shelters, baskets, and useful implements. All sorts of special skills developed, including recognizing the seeds, nuts, leaves and fruit which were safe to eat, probably by observing wild animals. Others must have explored their home area to discover resources of fish, and animal prey of different types, and learned how to hunt and prepare these for eating.

Medicinal plants were discovered long ago. Their preparation, drying, storage and use were in the hands of wise herbalists. Although we don't know exactly how they saw the natural world around them, our ancestors must have begun to alter their surroundings. By cutting off a branch, the tree is changed; by digging for flint stone to make tools, the land is reshaped; by using fire, whole areas might have been burned and habitats destroyed. As people developed more skills they also began to change the whole landscape. By noticing how the Sun and Moon shifted their rising and setting points along the horizon, and seeing patterns in the stars in the sky being altered by the wandering stars we know as planets, some sort of spiritual relationship was forged between people and the cosmos.

This earth/sky relationship seems to have been the impetus for another of our ancestral desires to change things. Markers were put up to show the Sun's position, and how it moved through the seasons. The wooden posts were later replaced by far more durable stones, and from then on simple stone circles and ellipses began to be constructed. The exact placement and mathematical accuracy of these ancient monoliths has lasted for 9,000 years in some cases. Not only did these sky-watchers move stones and tree trunks, they dug pits and huge ditches, raised embankments, mounds and linear features now called 'cursuses'. Thousands of these monuments have left traces in the ground that are shown up by modern scanning technology and patterns in crops during a drought. The skills and labour involved in making these ancient constructions was immense, considering the population was quite small at the time and the only tools they had were made of bone, wood or sharpened stone. We don't know what they believed or if they had the idea of Gods and Goddesses, but they obviously saw things in Nature that needed to be marked and perhaps celebrated. Traces of large feasts and fires have been unearthed, which implies that people gathered to eat and perhaps perform ceremonies. The remains of about thirty deer skulls which had been shaped into a sort of mask or headdress were found in the North of England and dated to the middle Stone Age.

Development of the Earth
As communities developed and people settled in one place they shaped their surroundings, building huts, animal pens and formed trackways as they travelled across the land. The large forests that covered much of the landscape were hollowed out into clearings and the timber used to make homes, boats, tools and trackways in the marshes. Gradually the grains we still depend on were planted in clear areas. New skills of grinding flour between stones, baking bread, creating decorated pottery and weaving were shared among communities. Treating animals' skins for clothing and tents, and

herding and taming cattle and horses showed other possibilities for developing new knowledge. It is hard to remember how clever and resourceful our ancient forebears were as so many areas of their knowledge have been lost. We don't know exactly why they set up rings of stones, carved ditches around them or placed other markers on the horizon, but it must have been important to link earth and sky, and to delineate the passage of the Sun, Moon and some stars and planets across the heavens. These ancient people began the process of reshaping the landscape which continues to this day.

There is nowhere in Britain where the natural earth has been left untouched by people. We think of old forests, moorland and coastal plains as wild places, yet each area will have been altered to make planting crops or keeping livestock easier. Humans have been changing the skin of planet Earth for thousands of years, destroying habitats of wild animals, birds and insects, altering the run of water courses, limiting fields with walls, hedges and ditches and building settlements and roads. This unthinking interaction with Nature has had terrible effects on many living things, causing them to become extinct. We may not be personally responsible for killing off butterflies and beetles, wild plants or wildlife, but each time we dig the garden we disrupt the micro-climate of many insignificant creatures and plants. Today when trees are felled or streams put into underground culverts, when hedges are ploughed out or structures built across natural wildlife corridors, we are doing harm. And now this thoughtless process of human endeavour is coming back to haunt us in the form of climate change, natural disasters and epidemics. We have changed Mother Nature and now she is changing us.

Advances in Technology

Each step in the evolution of agriculture, industry and transport has had an extreme effect on what was there before. From the development of Roman roads, Celtic hillforts, earthworks and burial mounds, through to redesigning the landscape to suit people in order to develop villages and towns – every change has disrupted Nature. People wanted to connect various places, at first

by footpaths, then packhorse trails, until finally the roads we recognize today were levelled and paved. As time passed, industries
developed, and the mining, smelting and casting of bronze tools
and weapons led on to the discovery of iron ore. This durable
metal required large amounts of wood and charcoal to burn in
order to refine it, so as well as creating pits and quarries, large
tracts of old trees were cut down. Once coal was found other
mines were excavated, and then canals had to be dug too, so large
heavy loads of ore, stone and coal could be moved around. At each
stage of industrial advancement, more of Nature was covered over,
or carried away from its original location. As the human population expanded, more food was needed, more cloth, more metals,
wood and stone for building, clay for bricks and pottery, were all
taken as expected benefits from Mother Earth. Industry brought
pollution of the air with smoke and fumes, and water with residue
from chemical processes. The seeds of climate change and atmospheric warming began hundreds of years ago. No one knew, as
their science was not able to understand the global picture, but
we know now.

With each advance, people were taken further away from their
rural roots, customs and country skills. When the railways came,
more and more workers were called from the farms and villages to
towns and cities to work in mills and factories. These folk had little
time for Nature, or for inner peace and contemplation. As well as
their bodies being bound by working hours, their minds and spirits
were starved of inherited knowledge and wisdom. However, people
are flexible and ingenious. In Britain they survived invasion by the
Romans, the Normans and the Vikings, all of whose influence was
relatively small. As each invader was eventually defeated or retreated
to their homelands, the original inhabitants continued with some of
the innovations the invaders brought, and ignored others. Some of
the invaders tried to force their Gods and Goddesses on the native
people, and again, some of these were accepted and woven into their
beliefs, while other faiths were ignored or rejected. Alongside the
Roman Gods and the fierce Norse deities were the ancient magics

of the invaders' traditions. They brought divining arts and healing skills as well as domestic architecture, luxury goods, weapons, pottery styles and boat building. Some of these were welcomed and gradually became part of the magical practitioner's craft. There were always midwives, healers, bone-setters, fortune tellers and wise folk hiding among the rural population. These cunning folk were never organized, never shared religious views or local festivals, but kept up their esoteric practices in the shadows.

The Influence of Mechanization

As time passed more new industries sprang up as railways made travel easier, moving raw materials and goods increasingly quickly. The laying of track cut through people's land, and the embankments, cuttings and tunnels severed natural wildlife corridors and blocked waterways. People could move further across the land, and fresh fruit, vegetables and grain could be transported in bulk to cities, and fish brought in from the coasts, so there were some benefits. But what was destroyed was the spirit of the landscape and the patterns of woods, fields and lakes were changed forever. The country folk saw huge engines chuffing across their fields, sometimes setting fire to ripening fields of grain, and shaking the foundations of their villages. Yes, new occupations were created, but the new heavy industry had a different rhythm to the slow ebb and flow of day and night. Workers became distanced from their natural roots and many customs, festivals, markets and celebrations which had united country-dwellers for generations were forgotten. However, in some countries people have managed to avoid the destructiveness of the modern world, remain in contact with their land, its Nature spirits, and give honour and gratitude to their home area. They still celebrate seasonal events, observe changes in weather conditions and give thanks for their ability to co-exist with Nature. Some free-thinking people now are taking heed of these important aspects of life and re-enact old traditions, realizing that they need to connect with Nature, their inner selves and the people around them.

In the last 200 years we have seen the development of the motor car and then the aeroplane and the factories that make them. Films, cinemas, and later television brought pictures to towns and cities and eventually to homes. Huge electronics factories turn out millions of screens, gadgets and handsets to meet the surging desire to own the latest technology. Little of this manic progress has bothered to consider the effect of pillaging the rare minerals and lands all over the world. Social contact has become electronic rather than face to face. Whole swathes of useful skills are being lost, traditional crafts are seen as out of date, and the vast amount of inherited knowledge about Nature is being forgotten. This is to the detriment of people, who are, after all, part of Nature. Children no longer recognize trees and plants, and the fruit and vegetables which still grow in gardens and allotments and parks. They don't know the rules of 'Conkers' or how to play 'Hopscotch'. If they see morris dancers outside a pub they do not realize such things hark back to old fertility rites or celebrations of harvests. They do not know that there is real magic outside books and films. People are being diagnosed as 'Nature deprived'!

The pollution caused by charcoal burning and metal smelting hundreds of years ago has been found locked up in European glaciers, and ice cores from Antarctica. Science is now showing us the effects of a thousand years of destructive activities, although the people who carried them out had no idea they were causing harm. Only in the last hundred years or so have investigators and ecologists begun to recognize the dire situation the Earth is in. Knowing there are many large problems is only the first step towards doing something to reverse these destructive activities before we all suffer. Not only are the climate, the weather, the water supplies, animal habitat and thence many species, plants and natural resources in deep trouble, but so are we. Our physical health, our mental wellbeing and our spiritual evolution is being stunted. Many people suffer from stress-related illnesses. Once our souls become sick or deprived of inner nourishment, the whole population become vulnerable to infection, as we all discovered to our cost with Covid 19 in 2020.

The Urgent Need to Combat Climate Change and Pollution

Humans are tough. We have survived invasions, wars and extreme weather conditions which wiped out food crops, or killed farm animals in years of extreme volcanic eruptions. Floods and wildfires and tsunamis, pandemics and plagues afflicted the world. The Black Death alone killed a third of the population in the fourteenth century. Later on, smallpox, cholera, malaria and all kinds of infections took their toll. These caused the population to shrink, changed the ways people lived, and so new types of medical cures were sought. Eventually we bounced back, increasing our population, and the effect we had on Mother Earth decade on decade. Only now are we starting to realize that action must be taken immediately. Because information can be transmitted instantly around the world, almost everyone has heard the fact the vast ice caps at the North and South poles are melting ever faster, potentially causing world-wide coastal flooding and erosion.

The other peril which is entirely the fault of humanity is the disaster of plastic pollution. No one realized at the start that this 'miracle' material would later on result in the deaths of countless sea creatures, the poisoning of river systems and the strangulation of water birds, seals and dolphins. It has been made all too clear that plastic in all its forms is a dangerous and deadly substance. What is worse is that most of us find it useful and very commonplace. Now that has to change. For a start all of us can really make an effort to correctly recycle all our waste products, especially plastics and metal cans. We can easily compost most vegetable greenery from the kitchen or garden and encourage our local council to collect and recycle it. Wasted food creates enormous problems including the production of greenhouse gases if it decays in refuse dumps.

To waste anything edible is a crime against Nature, when many people, even in the wealthy West, go hungry. Dumping food also wastes money, the time spent growing it, shipping it, packing it and buying it. Such waste devalues the work of the producers, and ultimately undervalues the fertile Earth herself. The old adage 'Waste not, want not' has to be at the forefront of our life styles. Treating food consciously may be a small thing but it can be a great factor in reducing harm to our whole world, and despite new tourist trips into space this is still the only planet we have. We are all responsible, it is our world, and now we know this we must act immediately. We must raise awareness in thought and deed, and where we are able to use the ancient arts of magic alongside electronic communications, we must share the message.

Nature is a Finite Resource

Now, more than ever before, we must recognize that we are part of Nature. If we harm the Earth, we eventually harm ourselves and those we love. All resources are finite so being greedy, taking more than a fair share, or hoarding deprives others, and clutters our own environment. We all need physical and mental and spiritual room to breathe and balance ourselves, on all levels. Regular meditation doesn't seem very exciting, but it opens doorways to inner sight, calmness and inspiration. For each problem there is an answer, and

magical thinking can often show us what it is. By living gently on this planet, really considering what we are doing, we can summon those unseen forces which can help to restore aspects of the Earth. We need to acknowledge our responsibility in this, become totally aware of the problems and difficulties and face them head on. Solutions can evolve. We have to live in hope, and believe this too will be altered for the betterment of everyone and all other living things, both seen and unseen. Through knowledge and education the first green shoots of restoration are showing and every one of us must treasure them.

Is this the Dawning of the Age of Aquarius?

For a long time astrologers and mystics have been predicting the coming of the Age of Aquarius, when the Spring Equinox sunrise falls in Aquarius instead of Pisces. (*See* Chapter 1 for explanation of the precession of the Equinoxes.) The Piscean Age of the Great Year was a time of mass movements, of authoritarian control and world religions. It was a time of conflict and rebellion, because not everyone wanted to be part of the 'one size fits all' generation. Pisces, a water sign of the Zodiac, was the 2,000 years or so of being expected to act like a school of fish, swimming in the same direction. Aquarius, an air sign, is about individual thought, independent action and originality.

In the past the change of Great Signs in the circle of the Zodiac might only have been recognized by the various priesthoods of the time. There was little worldwide communication to spread this knowledge as connections could at best happen at the speed of a sailing ship or a galloping horse. The ancient astronomers, who watched the movement of the Spring Equinox sunrise against a background of stars, would have gradually become aware that something was happening. Certainly developments in religion began with the coming of Jesus, and the spread of his message from the Holy Land. Some people accepted the gentle instruction to love one another, but like any new mass movement it was greeted with suppression and hatred. The new religion allowed both women and slaves to be baptised into it, so gaining a foothold on the spiritual landscape.

Many other major faiths in the East predate Christianity, including Hinduism, Buddhism and Zoroastrianism, to name a few. We are not influenced by these ancient faiths on the face of it, in Britain, although we have Indian shop-keepers, Chinese take-aways and the hundreds of doctors, nurses, care workers or dentists who follow these religions and help us. In the past there have been many conflicts and most of religious leaders went to war with other religious groups, causing countless human deaths worldwide. These holy wars continue to this day, setting neighbour against neighbour, land against land and adherents of one faith condemning all others. The simple spiritual messages have been lost in the lust for power over others.

Now we are facing a new challenge, not brought by a messiah or prophet, but by a tiny organism with no spiritual message at all – Covid 19. The whole Earth has been shaken by a new and different threat to life and society. For a time all our 'normal' freedoms were taken away or restricted. For a time we were forbidden to hug our children, comfort the sick and dying, marry with shared celebration and bury the dead with dignity and family reunion. We have been limited in space, confined to homes or gardens, yet made to distance ourselves from our loved ones and friends. Electronic communications are not the same as chats together over a cup of tea or a shared meal. Many people felt isolated and cut off from things that gave them pleasure, such as strolls along the coast, walks in the woods, even shopping for everyday things. So many areas of life had to be reconsidered, and concepts of what really mattered reconfigured. Many people found new supporters, struck up connections with strangers, and exhibited the best personal traits of kindness, sympathy and generosity in the face of an invisible enemy. No one asked for the great changes to happen, no one set out to upheave the entire world, but everyone is now having to live with the consequences of this health disaster.

Humanity has survived the destructive forces of Nature often, but these only affect one area on the face of the globe at any one time. Floods, fires, earthquakes, volcanic eruptions, tsunamis may all strike without warning, but there is usually somewhere to run to, to take shelter or to escape to a safer place. With plagues the opposite is true. Nowhere is safe, and the Piscean need to flock together is the wrong thing to do. In one way, we are all on our own, just as the Water Bearer, the symbol of Aquarius is alone, carrying the water pot to share with others. It is a symbol of individual giving, and everyone has a part to play. Humanity has survived for thousands of years, losing affinity with Nature and her rhythms. Also many subtle senses, intuition and awareness of the seasons have been lost in an electrically-lit world. New ideas, techniques and developments have followed. These days we have far more information to quickly deal with disasters, organize help, and eventually plan for the new patterns of life. We have access to transport, equipment, science and medicine, which our ancestors didn't have, but our priorities may be suddenly changed. Every day scientists and doctors are creating and refining vaccines, injecting them safely into millions of people around the world, and it is likely that this essential preventative therapy will be necessary for years to come if we are to limit this deadly contagion.

After the crisis of the Covid 19 pandemic, so many situations have changed. People live with the fear of new variants flaring up in case all the strict restrictions on movement, travel and gatherings are reimposed. No one likes changes that occur outside their own control, and when something happens on a large scale all sorts of negative emotions are generated. Even a small ordinary set-back can cause a feeling of loss, of disappointment or of anger. When a larger scale disaster happens with loss of life, transformation of the surroundings by fire, flood, tempest or earthquake, for example, rage against Nature, guilt at having survived or helplessness in the face of destruction will result. It is at this moment that the true strength of human spirit and Nature can take over.

Seeking Positive Solutions

It is essential to think about the positive steps that can be taken, help that can be offered in all sorts of different ways. When a new global threat occurs, there is no precedent to instruct our leaders, or a handy book of instructions for the general population. We are all in the dark until science and knowledge of our enemy reveal a way forward. Often there is confusion, and lack of guidance and outside assistance. The media may not be able to explain what has happened, and sometimes individuals are convinced it is only them, their local area or family that have been affected. It really is important to know that these events can occur on a vast scale, disrupting whole cities, countries or continents. It is not a personal attack on anyone, a plot to prevent your activities, or restrict your ability to go where you would like. Normality ceases and so each of us must take stock of the situation, seek out reliable information on what has happened and apply common sense to counter negative thoughts. There is lots of misleading or incorrect information being spread about. People are frightened, they are angry and often hit out, even when offered help, because they are encircled by their own negative experiences.

Recognizing this is the first step to change for the better. Close your eyes and in your mind's eye see what you can perceive. Maybe you can sense energies around you and aren't sure what they are; mentally ask for information from them. Subtle senses are very important when it comes to divination, healing, meditation and many other aspects of natural magic.

PART II

WORKING WITH THE ELEMENTS

5

THE ELEMENT OF EARTH

Stone is the foundation of our planet and the geology of the place you live will determine which sorts of plants will grow happily, how well the ground retains water, and how stable it is in times of flood or drought. The most obvious places to explore what lies beneath are often on the coast, where beaches may be made up of sand, pebbles or rock. There might be cliffs of white chalk or dark granite or basalt. Each kind of rock supports a different landscape. Seeing the land, feeling its energy, even from a small pebble, can be a strange awakening of the spiritual energies which are parts of a new or renewed relationship with Nature. This connection lies at the heart of spiritual ecology. Our interaction with each of the four elements of Earth, Water, Fire, Air, and sometimes Spirit or Aether, can form the basis for powerful natural magic.

First we should consider the Earth – it is our home planet and the basis upon which we live. There are three main environments to consider when we look about us. The most familiar is probably the urban areas in our lives, the built environment of houses, roads, shops, industrial premises, railways, airports and high rise buildings. These are artificial creations, some useful, some beautiful, and some ugly or derelict, but all seemingly inhuman and not parts of the natural world. But it is important to learn to look more closely.

If we are going to reconnect with the spirit of Nature it is to consider all landscapes, in a wider view, and the small things close to us. Looking at aerial photographs of towns and cities, it is possible to see green areas, parks, gardens, river banks, even green roofs and walls. A large percentage of the land in any town will be made up of individual gardens, waste land, allotments and public spaces, all of which provide homes for a vast array of wild creatures; plants considered by some to be weeds, trees, hedges and ponds. Every one of these has its share of small and larger wild mammals, birds, amphibians, insects and spiders. By getting to see and value these enduring examples of Nature in urban places we can discover wild aspects of our own life. Seeing a bright butterfly in a garden can lift the spirits, as can a Spring flower after a bitter Winter. Green-ness is good for the soul.

Some Areas of Knowledge are More Important

It is not necessary to be able to identify every bird, plant or tree to appreciate them as living things that share and enrich our planet. Just gaining insight into what things are enhances our knowledge of the world. Many plants have medicinal properties, and are often used in healing teas and tinctures. Trees may seem to be just big brown poles with leaves at the top, but the different varieties provided our ancestors with all kinds of useful timber to build homes, make tools, furniture, carts and fences. Each species of tree has special qualities. The oak tree is a host for all kinds of birds, insects, moths, butterflies, mosses and lichens. It was revered by the ancient Celtic peoples and the word 'Druid' may derive from *Derw* in old Welsh, so they may have gathered in oak groves.

Oak wood was used for roof timbers and boat building. Other trees like alder were used for bridge supports as alder wood hardens in water. Ash was used for resilient tool handles, hazel for making hurdles, and the structure of wattle and daub walls, as well as producing tasty nuts. Yews were used for making mazes, and the springy wood of their branches made into longbows to defend the realm. Dark-leaved yew can live for thousands of years; its foliage is

poisonous to livestock yet thrushes thrive on its sweet magenta berries. These eternal trees are often found in old churchyards, some of them pre-dating the Christian edifice, proving the site was special long ago. They are often quite magical.

Willow bark has been a traditional pain-relieving medicine for hundreds of years, and recent research shows it might have anticancer properties. Willow withies are used to make baskets and living walls along the banks of Dutch canals, as well as a recent application in bio-fuel. Rowan or Mountain Ash with its white clusters of flowers and rich orange berries has often been seen as a magically protective tree, so charms were made by cutting two twigs, binding them in a cross and hanging it indoors to guard the house. The berries can be dried and used as beads and in spells.

Elder, with its frothy cream blossoms and dark purple berries, is another protective plant, thought to be loved by faery folk who can be vengeful if their tree is cut down. The flowers can be made into a sparkling 'champagne-like' wine, and the dark Autumn fruits into an Elderberry Rob, a syrup useful against Winter colds. The dried twigs have soft centres and can be fashioned into rustic bead necklaces to ward off harm.

Birch trees have been tapped for their sweet sap by Scandinavian peoples in the same way that in Canada maple trees are tapped to make maple syrup. Their strong bark was used to make containers and canoes in North America, and their flexible twigs formed the traditional bristles of a witch's besom.

Many trees are grown for their fruit although often they have other more secret uses too. The apple when in blossom in April shows 'the Silver Branch' with its pale bark and scented flowers. According to John Matthews, in Celtic folklore the Silver branch was a Bardic token, allowing safe passage, and was a symbol of peace. It can be the passport to faery land, and more importantly, it also allows its bearer to return to the 'real' world. If you cut an apple in half crossways you will find a five pointed star or pentagram, which is a powerful magical symbol. Whereas the yew is a tree of immortality the apple is the tree of life with its familiar fruit and mystical twigs. Strong cider can be made from the sharper apples, as well as perry from pears. Plums and cherries, along with their wild cousins, the bullace, sloe and damson, produce small fruits more often used in jams and to flavour gin. Once you begin to explore the world of fruit trees, the orchards become magical places where it is easier to cross between our realms of those of legend.

Gardening Techniques and Uses of Trees

The art of forest gardening is becoming more popular, where plots contain fruit and nut trees, while below them soft fruits like gooseberries, raspberries, brambles, and currants of all kinds are planted as they tolerate shade. Among them roots and vegetables which grow quickly, and other herbs can be sown. If chickens are kept they can free range when the fruit isn't ripening and enrich the soil. This form of horticulture requires little digging and can be incredibly productive, even in quite small spaces.

With a bit of imagination even a town balcony or flat's window-sill can have a range of edible crops, especially herbs, right next to the kitchen. Tiny gardens and courtyards can be filled with deeper containers to grow beans, lettuces, radishes and tomatoes, especially the small varieties that are designed to thrive in pots, and deep sacks of compost can produce delicious new potatoes or carrots. It is hard to beat the satisfaction you get from having a meal that includes your own fruit or vegetables when you are able to share them with loved ones. Even weeds can be turned into enriching compost, and bees love their flowers.

Gardens should not need chemicals or artificial fertilizers if you use good growing mediums. Remember to water your plants in dry weather, ideally with collected rainwater, and respect and hon-our them and give mental thanks. The old skills of gardening pro-vide physical comfort, as well as calming the mind and enriching the spirit. Horticulture is used as a therapy, and doctors can now prescribe gardening for its health-giving qualities. Just looking at plants or flowers, or standing under a tree will bring magical and medicinal benefits.

There are dozens of varieties of trees in Britain that have useful or mystical connections and it can be a lifetime's work to learn them all. Some are not tall trees, but the kinds of shrubs used in tradi-tional hedges, like hawthorn or May, and blackthorn or sloe, both of which are used in herbal medicine. Writing in 1790, Edward Davies tried to link the names of various trees in Irish and Welsh with the names of the letters of their alphabets. Later on, the poet Robert Graves enlarged upon this research, discovering poems and old sayings about the importance of different trees at various times of the year, or their uses in country crafts. From this a whole form of divination has been developed, and picture cards, a bit like the Tarot have been printed. Graves knew that each month had a mystical name, just as there are a number of festivals celebrated throughout the year, and more recent authors have published works on the Celtic Tree Alphabet linking some of this information. It is another branch of research which draws on aspects of Nature and human awareness.

Even if you aren't able to get to flowering or fruiting gardens as much as you would like, just sitting still, with your eyes closed and imagining them can help. Using the 'mind's eye' is a powerful magical method because clearly imagining or remembering something can be the first step to making it happen. If you think about it, every created object, whether the plot of a book or the design of a garden or for a new car, began in someone's imagination. The inner process of a focused mind is essential to practical magical or spiritual work. The powers of Nature, the old Gods and Goddesses, saints and angels, are not often seen in our waking world, but by calling them up until they feel real is an important step. By 'seeing' these beings, we can communicate with them, ask for help, give thanks and engage them in actual magical change.

Creative Visualization

There is a useful art called 'creative visualization' which is used to guide a relaxed person on an inner journey to a place of beauty and calm. This can be a recollection of a real walk in the countryside or by the sea, or it could have been read in a book or seen on a screen. The idea is to focus completely on the journey, the sights, sounds, smells and feelings, taking you away from wherever you are sitting. This journey might lead to an ancient stone circle, a castle or a glade in a forest. In that place where the realms of mind and magic meet, new knowledge can be gained, inspiration found or insights into solving a problem can emerge.

This sounds simple, but it does take practice to be able to enter into the correct balance of relaxation and awareness to make it most effective. It costs nothing but time and concentration, and will pay dividends to anyone who masters this skill. You may meet the Earth Mother, the Green God of growing things or some deity from mythology or tradition.

The Importance of Farming

It is important to be able to see and understand the countryside. Looking from above, much of Britain shows a patchwork of different green fields, walls or hedges, rough moorland, mountains, rivers and woods. This is a working landscape. Each kind of field contains livestock or arable or table crops or orchards. The farmers who care for these great tracts of land really care about their patch of earth, their animals and the green environment. To people more familiar with towns, buildings and gardens, these places may seem alien and uncared for, and the livestock just seen as commodities to be raised then killed and eaten. This is often far from the reality.

Many farmers' families have lived at a particular place for generations, raised their children, built barns and cattle sheds, dairies and pig pens. To increase their farm's income, they have often turned to rural industries including cheese-making, processing wool and selling fresh milk or meat on site. This adds no food miles, and is ultra-fresh. They have bred cattle, sheep, pigs and horses with as much care and love as some folk do for their pets, and now farm llamas, emus and ostriches. Seeing that their animals are content, that the land is productive, and that the open environment is well tended as a natural resource, really matters to them. Often they have had to deal with their own disasters of animal diseases, floods and droughts, or the destruction of standing corn by rain or fire. Farmers are the backbone of the land, and their produce is essential to the wellbeing of all of us.

Climate change is having an adverse effect on the countryside which is becoming ever more desperate each year. Certainly we can choose what we eat, but a lot of the fruits and vegan options have to be brought from overseas, adding to pollution and food miles. Fresh, local, seasonal vegetables, meat, fish and grain do less harm to Mother Earth than some imported foodstuffs. The vegan staples of soya and rice do not flourish in our climate.

If cattle and sheep were removed from the land, it would become rough scrub, with brambles, bracken and weed trees taking over. It would not look like pictures of meadows full of rare wild flowers in all the colours of the rainbow that happy people can prance through under a blue sky. Farmers and stock-keepers are guardians of the land, whether they produce fruit and vegetables, milk and cheese, meat, eggs or grain for bread and beer. It is in their own interest to look after all aspects of their farms. During World War II the agricultural industry was encouraged to be more productive, enlarging fields by stripping out hedges, breeding different sorts of livestock and using more chemicals to do this. Afterwards as equipment got larger, fields were worked right to the edges, and even more walls and hedges were removed. In recent years the folly of this method has become clearer, as wind can blow fertile top soil into rivers, silting them up and adding fertilizer to water plants, which then choke the stream. This in turn blocks the waterways, which can then cause flooding. The whole land is part of a vast interconnected system that needs to be brought into balance. To some extent this is happening as science can assist farmers and landowners how to best value and protect their land.

Helping Mother Nature

Set-aside land at the edges of arable fields are being sown with seed-bearing wild plants to encourage birds, which also feed on insect pests. Hedges are being replanted or traditionally cut and laid so that birds and small mammals have nesting sites, and berries to feed on too. Beneficial insects and even bats are all doing their part in increasing fertility and eradicating harmful insects. Old dry stone walls are being rebuilt, offering homes for small mammals, which feed owls and birds of prey, as well as giving shelter to sheep and cattle on upland farms.

Scientists are helping farmers see their crops from drones and spot areas in a field which might need more nitrogen, for example, instead of flooding the whole field unnecessarily. Soil scientists are matching the actual land to the best things to grow there, and all sorts of experts and traditional country workers are sharing their knowledge to do the best they can. Even gardeners are trying to reduce the use of pesticides and weedkillers so that their plots are healthy, productive and beautiful. This is all-important because we too are part of the Earth; we breathe the air, eat the crops, and enjoy exploring the countryside. If the spirit of the land and its animals are well, this nourishes the souls of the people.

As most people grow up in towns and cities, we have become divorced from the countryside at large, and possibly don't give much thought to where our food actually comes from. Shops provide such a variety of fruit and vegetables all year round that we have lost touch with the seasons and the food they produce. We now need to reverse this, and learn exactly where what we eat comes from, and ask ourselves whether is it home-grown. Does it have to be flown across the globe, adding food miles and costs to our pockets and to the Earth? It has always been possible to grow things in gardens and allotment to feed ourselves. In the past people had little option in the ages before canning or refrigeration. Most people ate food in season, from the locality, either by growing it themselves or bartering with neighbours. We have become too soft, too greedy and too self-centred to realize what harm our strawberries at Christmas, exotic vegetables, palm oil and soya beans can be doing to other countries' land and people. We have to change our perspective on these things, and learn more about the crops and farmed produce in our own area. Even cities have regular Farmers' Markets, offering fresh produce, wines, preserves and cheeses from establishments within twenty miles of the market. You might be astonished at what is on offer these days.

Today if we buy from them we can ask the seller where their produce came from. It may force us to eat a different diet of in-season vegetables, local milk, cream and eggs, and try many of the dozens of local cheeses Britain produces. Most countries have specialities of which they are proud and these can be made anywhere if the ingredients can be found. Learn to be surprised if you find a farm shop that sells Jerusalem artichokes in Winter, or salsify from the coast, wild game from the woods and moors, and all manner of herbs. Our ancestors ate lots of the plants we consider weeds, like wild garlic, dandelions, fat hen, chick weed, sorrel and ground elder.

They would use many sorts of leaves in soups and salads, berries from wild shrubs in pies, and made preserves of all kinds of surplus fruit and vegetables.

Recent research shows that there is a greater variety of things in our diet, such as drinking fermented milk called kefir or yogurt, sauerkraut and kimchi pickled vegetables, which can can feed our interior flora, fighting infections and keeping us well. The science of our inner selves is being explored to bring us a healthier way of life, so it is up to each of us to care for and nourish our guts and our souls.

Feeding the Spirit

Food is an important part of our lives. Any practical witch or magician ought to be able to cook a variety of dishes from scratch, using local supplies. It is a way of bonding with friends and family and children, who ought to be taught to cook and understand where their fruit and vegetables come from. No child is too young to stir ingredients or prepare fruit or salad with a bit of help. This encourages young folk to try new things and to take pride in helping make a home-cooked meal. It is a sharing of produce and knowledge, and it is a sacrament of blessed gifts from Mother Earth. Starting to understand the cycle of land, produce and eating may be the first step towards reconnecting with Nature in a very visceral way.

We need to understand that there is nothing we possess that didn't originate from the Earth, even if humans have shaped it, shops have sold it and we feel it is ours. It is this alteration of natural things which has contributed to our divorce from being part of Nature. Humanity has mined minerals, changed the shapes of rivers, cut down forests, introduced alien crops and pests into pristine areas of the natural world, over thousands of years. Now we are paying the price. But it isn't quite too late. If we can change how we think and act, we can in small ways reverse some of the harm that has been done.

As well as food, our ancestors relied upon the Earth to provide tools for their survival. The oldest tools of all are stones chipped to make sharp edges for butchering meat or cleaning hides to fashion leather for clothing, carrying bags and thongs to bind things together. It must have taken wise people to discover which were the best sorts of stones to use, and where they could be found. The use of flint for fire-making and for sharp blades founded an early industry, and though in many places flint could be found on beaches, as it can to this day, the best, dark grey stones often came from mines dug into chalk, where layers of fine flints were excavated. Because this was a rare and valuable commodity, flint-working, or knapping, to split off very sharp shards must have been an important activity. British flint tools have been found a long way from the mines where the raw material came from, and were often buried in the graves of ancient people who were valued in their communities. Like the fire-makers and preservers, their work was vital.

Another sort of stone used for making blades is obsidian, which is a kind of black glass-like mineral which is ejected from volcanoes. This too is a precious resource with divine connections, as it was created by the heat of volcanic eruptions. It is often looked upon as a magical substance, and in some cases used to see into the future, as a scrying mirror. Like flint, it was used to make spear points and scalpel-sharp blades by ancient craftspeople.

Earth Patterns

To some people, the Earth is a living being, a Mother Goddess, and energy paths, interlinked sacred sites, holy mountains and sacred springs all connect us to ancient power sources. Shapes of hills and lakes, valleys and plains depict Earth talismans, such as Stonehenge, Avebury, Merlin's Mound and white chalk horses on a grand scale. In recent years mysterious crop patterns have been seen in fields, and though some people have admitted to making them, there have been other intricate and strange mathematical images found among the cornfields. There is some evidence that some force has affected the wheat stems causing them to fall into amazing shapes. Certainly to walk into such a crop circle feels very much like walking into a sacred space or magical circle. The geometry of both shining planets and mystical landscapes are real and may be perceived by the seeker, and they form powerful magical patterns.

6

THE ELEMENT OF WATER

The Four Elements are the symbolic basis of Western magic. Earth, Water, Fire and Air represent markers of directions in a magical circle, but they are also the essential components of life. We cannot live for long without water, we need the earth beneath us to live on, the air to breathe and energy, which is linked with fire, to exist. Ancient people recognized these concepts, and gradually they became associated with the four points of the compass, the seasons of the year, and most systems of occult practice pay attention to them, although different systems allocate them in different ways.

This can be confusing to new seekers who read a variety of sources but it is important to stick to one set of information until its principles are fully understood. Meditating on each of the elements, finding a symbol of it, allocating a direction, colour, season of the year, and finding a balance between them are all vital steps in practical magical work.

Water comes in many forms, both obvious as in the kitchen tap and more abstract as mist or Arctic ice. We all need to spend time near water outdoors if at all possible, whether it is a river, lake, the sea or a small woodland stream, and it is important to respect water, and know it can be dangerous. It is also good to learn to swim at an early age, for safety's sake.

Pictures of pools or waterfalls can be calming and uplifting, as can the sound of running water (unless it is rain coming through the roof!). Many people prefer to drink mineral water derived from ancient underground sources, often with a richer selection of natural chemicals than tap water. Few people in Britain these days rely on wells or springs for their water supply, but in past times these sources of refreshment were essential to the development of communities. They could also be the cause of local epidemics in cities if the local well became contaminated with cholera or typhoid. It is said London became a much more densely populated city than Paris because the Londoners drank tea or beer made with boiled water, thus killing infective agents, whereas citizens of Paris drank water or wine.

The Connective Power of the Sea

Going to the seaside for a holiday has been a common annual event since it was suggested that sea bathing and even drinking sea water could be good for you, several hundred years ago. Today people like to swim, surf or paddle in the water, but drinking it is not a good idea. Because the sea is tidal, the ebb and flow twice each day offers a magical energy which can be used. The ebbing waves in either the sea or a tidal river can be used to take away negative thoughts or concepts which need to be discarded. The tides are controlled by the Moon.

Because oceans are a part of the water cycle of evaporation into clouds and rain, wishes or spells can be placed in moving water to be swept away, or blessings and healing prayers can be sent out into the ocean. An old spell was to write a plea for healing on a leaf and drop it into an ebbing tide or an out-flowing river. It was considered to have magical influence right round the globe, because of the interconnectedness of the seas, and the idea that rain sucked up from them will eventually fall on most inland places, even deserts. There is a mystical Sufi saying 'Most people recognize that the falling raindrop unites with the ocean, but only the wise know that the ocean unites with the drop.' This means that no matter how insignificant something might be, like the raindrop, it can influence the entire planet. This may be how magic works – a small act on a large scale.

Because water appears in so many different places, it can be a great help with meditation. If you can look at the surface of a still lake or even a puddle, you will see reflections. Gazing calmly at this image can help you reflect upon a particular situation or mental problem. The dark water may ripple or in some way indicate an answer for you. The ancient magical art of scrying or crystal gazing probably began with wise folk discovering how the reflective surface of water can show glimpses of something, perhaps the future or a helpful symbol. Later scrying glasses were made of crystal carved into a ball, or black mirrors of obsidian (a natural glassy mineral) were used. A dark-coloured bowl of water in a dimly lit room can be a start, if you mentally pose a question and wait patiently for something to happen. There is a knack to scrying, which can be learned with practice and persistence.

Sacred Waters

Running water or ebbing tides can take things away, but a rising tide can bring in luck, healing, peace and comfort. It is by making a spiritual connection with the nature of water that many benefits can arise; after all, our bodies contain a large proportion of water and we are more likely to die of dehydration than of hunger. Water has been linked with the spirit or the soul for many thousands of years. Every sacred book mentions water, both as the sustainer of life, as a cleansing or blessing agent, or as something which enlivens the soul. In the Bible, in the book of Genesis, it is written that 'the Spirit moveth on the face of the waters'. In the well-known twenty-third Psalm, 'He leadeth me through green pastures, he maketh me to lie down beside still waters, he restoreth my soul…' takes the reader on a spiritual journey. Jesus is reported to have walked on water, to have appointed his disciples as 'fishers of men', and at a wedding, turned ordinary water into wine, a spiritual substance in times past.

In ancient Egyptian texts, the souls of the dead are guided to a place of waterways, and the Sun on the day-long travel from sunrise

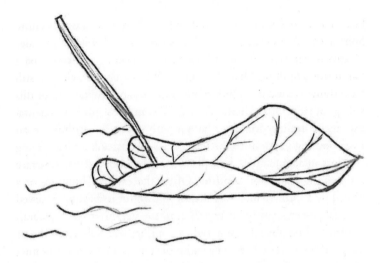

to sunrise is depicted as travelling on a boat along a river, accompanied by various Gods and Goddesses. The River Nile, which sustained their civilization, had its own God, Hapi, and there are many wonderful temples and sanctuaries close to its waters.

The Romans were adept at building aqueducts to carry fresh water to their cities from distant hillside springs, digging wells and making fountains in the streets for people to use. In Bath, known as *Aquae Sulis* in Latin, is where the primary hot springs in Britain rise and it was dedicated to the Goddess Sulis Minerva. This must have been a sacred and mysterious place long before the Roman invasion. Archaeological excavations have shown worked flints and pottery, which indicate that the hot waters were recognized and venerated.

The Celtic peoples in many parts of Europe made exquisite bronze shields, swords and mirrors, and seem to have cast these expensive items into water as offerings, as they have been recovered from the Thames, the Somerset levels, and many rivers and lakes in Europe.

Water as a Spiritual Gateway

Water was seen as a gateway to the invisible realms of the spirit below the ground, and the home of various deities from whom aid could be asked, or to whom thanks could be returned. If we are to become Spiritual Ecologists, one of the things we can work with in all sorts of ways is water. We can use it as a physical cleaning agent, so essential in times of ill-health and infection. We can use it to cleanse and bless things we use in esoteric work, and we can sprinkle it to purify a magical circle or meditation space. We can bless spring water and use it as a healing drink, or share it with others in a communion. Even pouring libations to the Earth is a way of thanksgiving.

Most ancient temples, holy places and churches had water nearby for cleansing and for baptism. Often the original building was placed by a spring which was already known for its healing water or magical powers. Any old map will show the streams, rivers and lakes of surface water, but they also indicate springs and wells from which people drew water before they had pipes and taps. There are dozens of holy wells, often with a guardian who might be a Pagan Goddess, a nymph or Christian saint. Even in cities it is possible to trace the courses of old rivers or locate the sites of springs or wells. This can be a fascinating area of research for many of these water sources were seen as holy or healing, and it may be possible to obtain such spring water for use in ritual or magical work if you know where to look. In many places there are actual sources of mineral water that you can collect, ideally in a glass or metal flask, as plastic can leach into any liquid it contains.

The Ill-effects of Pollution

Water is a world-wide precious resource which is under threat from climate change, overuse or waste and pollution. It has become clear that most oceans, rivers and even tap water can be contaminated with chemicals, and widely with plastics and micro-plastic. Nearly all the plastic ever made is still in existence, buried, dumped or degrading into smaller and smaller particles, on land and in the waters. These microscopic pieces can be mistaken for food by animals in the sea, which ingest them and are harmed or pass this pollutant up the food chain to fish and eventually to us. When water is polluted, it is then harmful instead of healing.

On land minute fragments of plastics and other human-created chemicals get washed into waterways, and can be absorbed into food crops, fruit and vegetables so that we end up eating them, or inhaling them in the atmosphere. Larger pieces of plastic choke birds, entangle their legs or wings and can lead to protracted and painful deaths. The careless, thoughtless discarding of a plastic wrapper or drink can ring carriers can cause great harm to the natural world. One thing we can all do is carefully dispose of any non-biodegradable materials, or better still, not receiving them in the first place – after all, fizzy drinks aren't good for you and can make you fat! We have to learn that even a tiny trivial action or inattention can be a catalyst for destruction.

It is this deeper awareness of degradation of the natural environment by humans which is leading to a greater understanding of everything we do with the world at large. Some excellent positive changes have begun to happen, from people taking it upon themselves to pick up litter, cans and plastic in their own street to mass collections in public places. Volunteering, either officially at an organized event, or spontaneously alone or with friends to litter-pick or to tidy up a neglected place can be incredibly rewarding on all sorts of unexpected levels. Clearing a beach or stream bank of discarded waste can be seen as a spiritual act, helping Mother Nature, making human and wildlife friends, and gaining a feeling of achievement. We need to do all we are able to in these kinds of situations, and become active guardians of the wild and open spaces. We also need to take care of our own inner beings.

Water and Feelings

Water is often associated with emotion, which can seem to spring from nowhere, bringing tears to your eyes, whether of joy or sorrow. The sight of a dewdrop on a flower petal, the smell of rain after a drought, the sensation of floating if you swim in the sea, or drag your fingers through a warm bath, all indicate the watery emotions. Even the pulse of our liquid blood, or the way our mouths water if we taste or smell something delicious, shows how important this liquid aspect of our beings is, even if we seldom think about it.

As our pulse beats in rhythm to our hearts, so do the tides of the sea ebb and flow at the attraction of the Moon. The Moon's phases are important in magical work for the waxing and waning of her light in the sky gives energy to spells and charms, encouraging things in the waxing phase, and releasing things with the waning light. Some people are aware that their own feelings change through the monthly cycle of the moonlight, sinking inside themselves as the light fades and reaching out and becoming wilder as the Moon grows full.

The Holy Grail

A powerful symbol associated with water is that of the Holy Grail. This mythical vessel was described as the cup used at the Last Supper of Jesus before his crucifixion. Western legends have many tales of older cauldrons and chalices, sacred swords or other relics. In some versions of the Grail story it is described as a stone which fell from heaven and has magical powers. In the Arthurian legends Merlin the magician asks King Arthur to get his knights of the Round Table to go on a quest to find the Holy Grail because the land has been laid waste. This can well be seen as a metaphor for the state of the planet in the twenty-first century. Now pollution, deforestation, mining, over-population, and the expansion of cities, roads and railways have eroded vast areas of natural land, destroying habitats and dispersing people.

We really need the healing power of the Holy Grail now because it can be a symbol that can revitalize this modern wasteland. Because no one knows what the Grail is, as a magical artefact it can take many forms, from a physical stone, a cup or cauldron, to a concept or instruction. Whatever it is, it has to hold water. Alabaster can be carved into goblets, for example, and rain or dripping water can hollow out even the hardest stone. Water collected from hollowed sacred stone structures is attributed to healing power.

The Quest for the Grail is deeply rooted in western magical tradition, and our individual journey to wisdom and healing can be part of this eternal search. The Holy Grail is a container and it shapes that which it contains. Water is an element that needs to be captured in something or it flows away uselessly. Similarly we are also containers of spiritual wisdom and intelligence, which is shaped by how we think and act. So it is important that we consider what we are doing, and the consequences of any action.

Water always flows downhill, seeking through streams and rivers to join the sea, but excess water caused by rainstorms and tsunamis will flood the land, washing away homes and buildings. Because most cities are near watercourses, either rivers, from which their water was originally derived, or near the coast, most towns and cities are vulnerable to sea level rise. The faster melting of ice sheets and glaciers is raising sea levels in ever-increasing amounts, and severe storms or continuous rainfall are affecting many parts of the world. Whole countries are at risk, including the Netherlands and Bangladesh, and all low-lying or geologically unstable littoral areas are being threatened.

People have tried to counter the rising tides but eventually the protective sea walls or concrete reinforcements are undermined and washed away. Sand is deposited in other places, and shingle banks shift, becoming hazards to ships all the time. These forces are beyond our personal control, but it is essential that we are aware how dangerous some coastal regions can be, and that the power of a flood or a rip tide near the beach can carry us away. Even cities like London, embraced by the powerful River Thames, is in danger as much of it is close to water level, and lots of the infrastructure, like the Underground is liable to flooding.

7

THE ELEMENT OF FIRE

Fire is another basic element of Nature which we need to understand for it has many uses in life and in magic. Possibly fire was the first 'tool' used by ancient people, originally discovered in lightning strikes on dry wood or grass. It was a rare and wonderful occurrence, and people learned to nurture small flames from Nature before they found ways of making fire for themselves. It was seen as a gift from above, a source of wonder, awe and worship. It is for this ancient reason that most religions acknowledge the sanctity of fire, using candles in their churches or temples or perpetually burning lamps. Many ancient gatherings involved bonfires or torch-lit processions, as they do to this day.

Our ancestors found that fire scared away predators, it could warm an enclosed space, and branches could be shaped by fire into sharp and hard points to make digging sticks or hunting spears. Gradually the uses of fire expanded to bringing light on a burning branch into dark places. Cooking on hot stones provided a new sort of diet, with plant and meat and fish being made more palatable and nutritious by heating. In order to cook, pots were needed and perhaps the womenfolk or children near the fire pit or hearth discovered that clay could be shaped and then baked to make containers. Museums all over the world display early bowls and jars and lamps. From the shape, the material and the way they are made, their age and that of a settlement can be determined. Some examples are extremely old.

Catching Fire

At first people had to rely on Nature to find fire, whether from lightning or combusting marsh gas, so the flames were precious and needed to be nurtured and fed. Somehow they found that striking two flint stones together caused sparks, which could ignite dry grass or bark. Later fire was made with a 'fire drill', whereby a stick was turned by hand on to a 'hearth' of harder wood to make sparks. Flint, which in some languages is called 'firestone', is also the raw material of many blades, scrapers and drills.

Today we do not have so many open fires or burning lamps as our ancestors, although some houses have wood-burning stoves, and it is nice to have candles to light up a dinner party. Gardeners occasionally have bonfires and there are still Bonfire Night celebrations in November, when pyrotechnic displays send fireworks into the sky. It is likely that this event, now connected with the Gunpowder Plot and Guy Fawkes' attempt to blow up King James I and the Houses of Parliament in 1605, marks a much older Fire Festival. November was considered by some as the start of the magical year, after Hallowe'en, so gathering round a bonfire to celebrate the successes of the year, to trade cattle, sheep and other handicrafts, was a common custom. Certainly the coloured modern fireworks were not available, but certain nuts including horse chestnut conkers can go off with a bang if thrown into a bonfire.

Fire and Divination

There are traditions of roasting chestnuts at this time of year as a form of divination about future events. A question could be asked and two chestnuts corresponding to 'Yes' and 'No' were put on the griddle. Whichever burst first gave an answer.

Other forms of Fire divination, which are used today, include 'Talking to a Candle' and wax divination. To talk to a candle, you can place one in a secure holder and stroke it with a magical oil in one direction. After a while the candle will start to feel different. You can give it a name, but be respectful. Light the candle and watch the flame to be sure it isn't in a draught. You may be surprised that when you speak to the flame, using the name you have chosen, it seems to respond, trembling or stretching, swaying or shrinking. You can invent a code, and ask it questions ideally with yes/no answers, allowing time for it to respond. See what happens. When you finish, say 'Thank you' and snuff out the flame. It is not magical to blow out a candle flame as breath is a sign of life, so pinch it out or use a snuffer. All manner of life has to be respected, even a living flame.

Wax divination is more random as it relies on personal interpretation of shape and form. In this some wax (old candle ends with the wicks removed are quite good) melted in a clean pan is quickly poured into a vessel of cold water. A blob or an obvious shape will result, which can be seen as an omen. (There are several other forms of interpretation of random shapes, like clouds, the smoke of incense either sticks or grains burned in a censer, or ink blots on folded paper for example.) Traditionally the diviner would prepare by meditating and perhaps blessing the candle, or the incense or the ink first. By being in a quiet state of mind and still position of your body, a clearer result will occur. Learning to be mindful, patient and focused are essential techniques for any sort of spiritual, magical or divinatory activity. Being out in Nature will help you embrace this knowledge.

Dangers of Fire

In recent years fires have been causing devastation in many countries due to climate change. Prolonged droughts have led to areas of forest or scrub, or even ripening corn, to catch fire. A small local blaze can swiftly spread across a whole tract of moorland, dry hillside and forest in minutes, and flames can move faster than a person or an animal can flee. Homes, farms and woodland have been and are being turned to ashes, along with cars, house contents and all the infrastructure. Electricity, water and gas pipes are destroyed and so whole areas are cut off by burning and by lack of communication. In many burned places there is no surface water with which to quench the conflagration so helicopters and planes have to bring it from lakes or the sea. They also drop chemical fire suppressants, which can be harmful to the trees and the land below in the future. If you are having a barbecue or a bonfire be very careful to ensure it is properly put out at the end, especially if you are away from home. A hot spark is enough to set fire to a whole village, and a carelessly untended cooker or bonfire can burn your house down. If you encounter a fire where it shouldn't be, call the Fire Brigade, for everyone's sake. Even candles can fall over and set fire to your furniture!

If you do get burned, run the affected area under the cold tap for at least ten minutes or immerse it is cold water. Learning First Aid is a magical art, and it could save your life or those around you. No such skill is ever wasted.

8

THE ELEMENT OF AIR

The fourth element used in terrestrial magic is that of Air. It is essential for our life, is invisible and is all around us. It contains various gases including nitrogen, oxygen and carbon dioxide. It is our breath and is often symbolized in magical work by burning incense, whose upward-drifting smoke carries prayers and incantations towards heaven. We mostly become aware of air, not when it is still, but when there is a breeze or wind. Many ancient peoples had a deity or spiritual being associated with wind, for example the Greeks had four, Boreas, Notus, Eurus and Zephyrus, blowing from the North, South, East and West. There was a God of the winds called Aeolus, to whom Aeolian harps, with strings that vibrated when the wind blew, were dedicated.

Air can power instruments other than those used in music. For example, windmills have been used for many hundreds of years for grinding corn into flour or crushing coloured stones for paint. Today wind turbines are used to generate electricity by harnessing air currents to turn huge sails. Often these enormous structures are set in the sea in groups or on open countryside, called windfarms. It is expected that this new source of energy, which is considered carbon neutral, will become even more widely used around the world.

Unfortunately, changes in the world's climate will also make gales and tornados more frequent, and these can blow away whole houses.

Sounds are transmitted through the air when we hear them and when we speak or sing, for example, we are using our breath to project the message, so air is associated with communication. Many kinds of vocal sound have been part of the magical tradition for centuries, from the singing of hymns and invocations to call for divine help, to rhythmic chanting which can cause changes in human consciousness leading to oracular or healing effects. Learning different techniques of singing can be very helpful as being with a choir or sharing incantations in a ritual is empowering and brings a sense of community. Many kinds of music have magical or spiritually uplifting effects on people, and are sometimes used in esoteric rituals as well as church services.

The Importance of Breathing Properly

Breathing is used in many traditions as an aid to meditation, sometimes combined with physical postures, or as a means of slowing down and concentrating. Counting slowly to inhale, holding your breath for a few pulse beats, and exhaling slowly often helps if you feel stressed. Choose a pattern of eight breathing in, hold for four, breathe out for eight and hold out for four. Repeat this pattern for several minutes for the best effect. You can pick longer or shorter patterns to suit your own abilities. Often the slower you can do this the more calming benefit you will achieve. Always concentrate on being relaxed in body but inwardly focused in mind.

An Exercise in Hand Breathing

This is a simple exercise in breathing which can be very calming and energizing.

Hold your left hand in front of you, palm facing you and fingers spread out. With your right forefinger slowly begin to trace the outside edge of your hand, from the wrist up the edge of your thumb. As you do this breathe in. As you trace the tip of your thumb, hold

your breath, then breathe out as you go down the other side of your thumb. Then breathe in as you trace the edge of your first finger, hold your breath at the finger tip, and breathe out until you get to the bottom of that finger. Then go on to the middle finger, breathing slowly in, hold at the tip, and breathe out going down. Do the same for your ring finger, breathing in as you go up, and out as you stroke the outside, down to the joint of the little finger, breathe in, hold and out, tracing the edge of your hand down to the wrist. Hold your breath out until you get to the base of the thumb when you slowly repeat the tracing of all your fingers. You can do this with your other hand if you like. The idea is to do this as slowly as is comfortable, all the time breathing calmly, and being aware of the touch both of the tracing finger tip, and of the edge of the fingers being stroked. Repeat at least three times. Once you get used to this 'hand breathing exercise' you will find it useful in stressful situations or if you can't sleep.

As you practise this, become aware of the shape and feel of your fingers, stretch and bend them, so that they remain flexible. Hands have always been important to humans being their first tools, and the shape and uses of them are what sets us apart from other clever creatures. Using touch has many uses in natural magic, for through our finger tips we are able to connect with other aspects of Nature.

Spiritual Senses of Touch, Hearing and Taste

If you can, go to a tree, feel and smell the bark, the leaves, the twigs and sense how upright it stands, even in strong winds. Try touching other plants, herbs and flowers and imagine you are finding them for the first time. Even if all you can get to are vegetables in the kitchen or cut flowers in a vase you can explore the varied textures, scents and energy. Even house plants benefit the air indoors. Then close your eyes and in your mind's eye see what you can perceive. Can you sense energy or life force? Do you get the impression of colour or shape, or even the setting where the plant came from? Such subtle senses are very important when it comes to healing, blessing a magical talisman or feeling the magical energy in anything.

Listening too is a magical skill which is linked to the element of air. Just being quiet wherever you are and paying attention to any sounds around you helps to focus and relax your mind. Out of doors you may hear birdsong or the whisper of the wind in the trees, the trickle of a stream or, if it is very quiet, even the beat of your own pulse. Sometimes when you are meditating you may hear voices or music and may need to pay attention to them. Many musicians are inspired by otherworldly tunes, sometimes visiting sacred places to listen for them. Inspiration, the act of breathing in, is a term for acquiring knowledge, often expressed through art, poetry or writing. When such unexpected information comes to you, it is as if you have inhaled guidance or wisdom.

Our senses of smell and taste are very important both as givers of pleasure and as alerts and warnings. The smell of smoke in a building can warn you of a fire, and so save your life, the disgusting smell of rotten food can help you avoid food poisoning. However, the pleasant scent of flowers or of incense can be used to awaken feelings of pleasure or even memories of happy events in the past. Because our nose is close to our brain, the sense of smell is very powerful so often a whiff of something we recognize from childhood can evoke strong memories.

Using Magical Scents

Incense is often used in magical work, and is specially blended for each ritual purpose. Although many kinds of incense grains, joss sticks and perfumed oils may be bought from lots of places, it is not always possible to know what they are made of, and some people can be allergic to their smoke. In the same way, room freshener sprays can affect some people adversely. Many of these things are artificial and could contain harmful substances. Like many of the practical skills associated with occult work, the arts of blending individual incenses can be learned. Usually to get good results from your blend, which is burned on special charcoal blocks in a censer, you will need three things. One is a gum or resin like frankincense or copal, something woody such as chips of apple or pine wood to help it burn, and flower petals, twigs or other scented dry materials associated with your ritual's purpose. These different substances all have planetary or magical connections, which have to be learned by studying 'Tables of Correspondences'. These lists show each herb, colour, flower or tree, gemstone, day of the week and esoteric associations for each planet or element. There are quite large books showing all the possible connections, including Gods and Goddesses from different ancient pantheons, phases of the Moon and so on. Like much of modern spiritual development, it is a lifetime study.

The Value of Spiritual Nutrition

On the matter of taste, which is actually very closely linked to the sense of smell, everyone will have their preferences. Some people like sweet things, others prefer sour or bitter tastes; most of us have individual likes and dislikes when it comes to selecting food. Many of these choices are learned at an early age, so if no one makes an effort to introduce children to a wide selection of fruits and vegetables and other important food groups, they will grow up with limited preferences which can be harmful to their long-term health. Cooking and sharing food is a kind of communion and being able to produce a meal for friends and family is a valuable skill. Obviously it may be a physical gift of nourishment, but it also is a spiritual process too. Most religious traditions have a custom of communal meals, as celebrations, festivals or commemorations. Knowing where fruits come from, how best to prepare vegetables, especially if you are able to grow some of these yourself, is so beneficial. Planting, nurturing, harvesting and tasting plants and then sharing the produce feeds the body, the mind and the spirit for all who can experience it.

Sky Divination

The air that surrounds us and is the medium of so many sensory experiences is also the harbinger of future events. There is an ancient tradition of weather witching. Some people believe that by watching a small Summer cloud in a clear blue sky and focusing their attention on it, they can split it, and then dissolve it into nothing. Trying too hard can give you a headache or stiff neck, and always be sure you are not looking towards the sun, as you can damage your eyesight. In the past sailors who relied on wind to power their ships were supposed to visit weather witches to buy knotted string so that by untying one knot they would get a breeze, by undoing the second knot they would get a stronger wind, and by loosing the last knot they would bring on a gale.

By watching the clouds in the sky, the direction of the wind and the colours at sunrise or sunset it is possible to predict weather patterns. 'Red sky at night, shepherd's delight; red sky at dawning, shepherd's warning' is a familiar saying. Low cloud of gold and scarlet in the evenings indicate high pressure and settled weather, but ruddy sky after dawn shows rain approaching. Different wind directions also show weather trends. 'When the wind is in the east, it ain't no good for man nor beast' goes one old saying, as does 'When the north wind doth blow, then we shall have snow'. Rainbows are thought to promise hope, and are used as symbols by many charities and ecological movements. Watching the sky for these portents, or allowing the breeze to blow away mental and spiritual cobwebs can improve many people's moods.

Country people have always observed the wind and the sky, the sun rise and sun set long before there were weather satellites in the sky, or meteorologists to interpret the electronic signals as omens about climate and atmospheric conditions. The folk who relied on the land for sowing crops and harvesting found their whole lives depended on reasonable conditions to provide Winter feed or fruit and vegetables in season. Learning about the weather and how it affects you now is just as important, as change in air pressure can increase anxiety, or make you feel happy. Become aware of these subtle signs in the sky.

9

THE FIFTH ELEMENT

The fifth element sometimes referred to in magical texts is that of Spirit, or Aether. This is an invisible, balancing force, symbolized by a light, a single point at the centre of the circle, or another sacred object. The four elements of Earth, Water, Fire and Air can be experienced, seen and attributed to the four directions, where they may be allotted symbols like stones, cups, lit candles and scented flowers, for example. Sometimes the practitioner is the representative of Spirit in the middle of the magical circle, and the elements are placed around. The centre is the balance point on which the turning four-spoked wheel spins. A standing human being can represent all the elements.

Becoming the Elements

Here is a simple exercise for relaxation and focus. Stand upright in a clear space, in or out of doors, and consider your feet. These are the Earthly roots that tie you to the planet. Wiggle your toes and imagine how strongly your feet support you. You are rooted in the past and the Earth beneath you nourishes you, while its rocks offer stability and endurance. Your legs are the trunk of a tree, able to sway in the winds of destiny, but will always symbolically connect you to your base and foundation.

When you consider the cup made by your hipbones, think about Water. This is the part of the body with your 'water works', your bladder and kidneys, and for women your womb, but magically the cup of your pelvis is a symbol of the Holy Grail, the centre of emotions, feelings of love and of healing. Allow yourself to consider your connection with water, in your blood as liquid, and as a source of ever flowing life, echoing to your pulse beat. Think of ebb and flow, of storage and release. All sorts of watery and cup-like ideas may occur to you.

Continue up your body and you come to the Solar Plexus, the seat of the fiery Sun in your belly. Here is the place of energy driven by your heart, pumping the life-giving blood around your whole being. Some ancient peoples thought that the heart was the seat of the soul; however nowadays most people associate the heart or a heart-shaped symbol as a token of love. Think about who you love and how that emotion is expressed. Do you actually say 'I love you!' to anyone? Do you love yourself? If you don't love and respect yourself, how do you expect anyone else to do that?

Moving up again you will encounter your chest and throat where your lungs and breathing systems function, your direct connection with the Air you inhale and exhale. Here is another place where forces ebb and flow. Proper deep breathing, from the bottom of your lungs is calming and energizing. As you stand, stay relaxed and try to draw air deeply inside you, expanding your belly, as well as your chest. Breathe out fully and pause, and then inhale again. See how this makes you feel. Air is not only needed to bring in oxygen but it provides the medium of speech, song and chant for communication with other people but also with other-worldly beings. Your ears are also connected to these sound systems, as the other side of speaking is listening, hearing music or just being aware of the noises of Nature. Actually hearing what is around you, or what someone else is trying to say, is a real art, often blotted out these days by headphones supplying artificial sounds. Teach yourself to listen.

Rising through your head, the centre of your intellect, source of memory, creativity, and undirected bodily functions, you come to the crown of your head. Here you are in contact with the divine spirit, your 'Higher Self' and the seat of wisdom. Imagine a silver thread lifting your head, straightening your spine and connecting you to the centre of the heavens above you. Through this slender channel may flow light and love and knowledge. It is the spiritual cord through which you can experience the wonder of Nature, communicate with invisible forces and draw nourishment to your soul. Become aware of the spiritual power all around you.

Stand still for a few moments allowing this experience, which can be quite strong, emotional or energizing, to settle within you. When you are ready, draw down the balancing light, through your crown, into your lungs, as a healing stream, then down to your fiery heart centre, down into your cupping hips and pelvis, and into the tree-like trunk of your supporting legs to your rooted feet and allow the energy to flow out to the Earth. Make sure you feel steady and grounded as this is a powerful magical exercise. If it seems too much to begin with, try it sitting down, or work on each elemental section in turn. Always take a couple of deep breaths and allow any energies to ebb out so you do feel grounded before going onto another task.

The Value of Spiritual Exercises

Throughout our life's journey, we will encounter many events and occasions of joy and difficulty. There will be successes and losses, but as the cycle of seasons turns we will have opportunities to learn and develop as human beings. Each experience will provide a chance to explore and to reconnect with our minds, bodies and spirits. We will be among loved ones at many of these feasts and festivals, but sometimes we may be alone, feel lonely and lost. By discovering arts of meditation, contemplation and creative visualization, these challenging times may offer new insights and possibilities. Try sitting still and looking inwards to a place of calm, becoming aware of your breathing, slowing it down and taking conscious control, and by breathing to a set, slow rhythm you will feel balanced and poised. If you relax, but feel around your body, bit by bit, you may discover areas of tension, and by acknowledging these, release them. Gently stretch, mentally reach out and allow your spiritual being to expand and explore. A good way to achieve physical relaxation is to tense and then let go of sets of muscles. Everyone has some tense spots as any masseuse would tell you.

Directed Relaxation

Sit upright on a firm chair with your feet on the floor, and your hands resting on your lap. Concentrate on your toes and clench each muscle you can, hold it for a count of five, and let go. Next flex your ankles upwards for five, and let go. Then work through your calves, and knees and thighs. Tense each area, fully concentrating on it, and then after a count of five really let go. You may need to press down on the chair or pull your legs together to get at each area. Clench your buttocks, then your stomach, and your ribs, which may involve pressing your arms to your sides for a count of five, and relax. Next work on your shoulders, and your neck, which are common areas of retained tension. Gently roll your head down and around, never forcing it, five times in each direction. You may hear crackles and find some aspects of the movement stiffer. These will iron out if you work on it. Go right round in both directions, letting your head roll gently.

Next pay attention to your hands, clenching your fingers and relaxing them five times. Spread your fingers and then curl them one at a time into loose fists five times. Push your elbows into your sides and hold and release. Take five really deep breaths and let them out slowly. Finally screw up your face and relax, frown and release, clench your teeth gently then stretch your mouth open as in a yawn and let every part of you relax. Feel mentally for any remaining tensions, taking your time, until every part feels as loose and calm as possible. Try this when you can't get to sleep, and before the meditation, visualization or any other magical exercises.

PART III

THE SPIRAL OF TIME – DISCOVERING THE RHYTHMS OF THE YEAR, ITS FEASTS AND FESTIVALS

10

Spring, the Awakening of the Spirit World

Traditionally every part of the year had its tasks, its festivals and the revealing of new experiences. Today we don't usually get called in to help with the harvest, or scatter seeds on the fields. We don't herd sheep, milk cows or plough the land, but our lives are still affected by the changing seasons. To awaken a sense of spiritual wellbeing here are some suggestions to work with through the passing months.

In Spring we recognize the first bright flowers, the snowdrops, primroses and daffodils in gardens and parks. There are many hundreds of kinds of plants, flowers, weeds and herbs all around us, whether in a city or the countryside. Perhaps you already know most of those you see, or realize that you can't put a name to them. You can learn to recognize a plant, revel in its beautiful blooms, acknowledge its use as a culinary or medicinal herb or edible vegetable, so forming an inspiring link with Nature's bounty. Plants provide a vast array of study material and inner delight. Even a few minutes actually looking at any flower, smelling its scent, touching its petals and considering its colours can provide a brief mental space in which to unwind. Every part of Nature reflects our human nature.

Spiritual Reassessment

It can be useful, at any time of the year, to take a brief break to look at your self. Just for a few minutes, find a place where you can sit still. Close your eyes, and focus on your breathing. It is important to learn to breathe deeply and regularly, concentrating just on the feeling of health-giving air flowing in through your nose and into your lungs. Hold it in for a short time then gently breathe out through your mouth. It is important just to experience these sensations. As you continue to take thoughtful breaths, allow the rest of your body to relax. Repeat these deep, slow breaths for several minutes becoming aware of what you are feeling. Focus inwardly and be in the moment, devoid of other concerns. Centre your thoughts on being

your 'true self', calm, strong and growing more healthy. This is one of the many techniques called 'Mindfulness' and it is an important step on the path of spiritual awareness and connection with Nature. Allow the outer world to flow back into your perception and continue to seek knowledge from the plants, flowers, herbs and green things around you.

Connecting at Candlemas

We often forget that many 'wild' plants were once used as food, for dyeing cloth, weaving baskets or as healing herbs. During the early months of the year it can be a good time to refresh the connection with the green and growing world. Just watching the gradual changes as the coldest weather relents and the first green shoots begin to appear can be uplifting to the spirits. It is a time of promise and potential. In some Pagan faiths, the start of February brought the festival of Imbolc, signified by the birth of the first lambs, or when the hours of daylight were enough to get through work without having to light a lamp. The second of February is celebrated in the church calendar as Candlemas, the feast of St Blaise, when a year's worth of candles were blessed. Some others honour Brigid, a poet, worker in metals and healer, by weaving reeds into a St Bridget's Cross. This four-spoked design symbolizes balance and harmony, the turning of the seasons, the four cardinal directions and the four elements.

Easter

Easter in March or April is a time of renewal and rebirth, with its associated symbols of eggs and chicks. The date for Easter Sunday is still set by the Moon, which is why the timing of this holiday moves. Easter Day is the first Sunday after the full Moon after the Spring Equinox (when day and night are equal in length), so it is always during a waning Moon. Some Pagans mark it as a time of balance of light and dark, a turning point of the natural year, with rituals at ancient sacred places.

The Spring holiday is a good time to explore awakening Nature, feel the fresh breeze and, with every day, try to discover something new about the world around you. It is not just a time to hunt for chocolate eggs, but to seek out the signs of a new season, and the opportunities it brings to renew your personal connection with the outside world. A simple slow walk along a waterway, by a lake, or even the banks of a city canal will show a plethora of plants and herbs, and at this time of year many ornamental gardens are opened to the public. Even a visit to the fruit and vegetable aisle of a supermarket will show the seasonal changes.

As the Spring progresses, the colours of the flowers change, from snowdrop white to primrose yellow, azure bluebells and then the pinks, mauves, purples, golds and creams of many wild flowers. In gardens the colours are even brighter as Spring flowering shrubs are dusted with white or pink. The first of the fruit bushes show their blossoms and the green leaves and lawns become verdant and lush. All around Nature is showing us a terrestrial rainbow, from park to roadside, from garden to country lane, from field to orchard. Being in these places can be truly uplifting.

May Day

The next old festival, at the start of May is called Beltane, 'the good fire', when cattle were driven between two bonfires of special herbs to ensure their health as they moved to Summer pastures. The hawthorn came into flower, its scented blooms promising fertility, and its fresh greenery, called 'bread and cheese', could be eaten as it contains many minerals and vitamins, after Winter's dearth. There is a saying 'Cast not a clout 'til May be out', meaning don't change to Summer clothes until these white flowers are seen, or perhaps until the end of the month of May.

Often at this time there is a real upsurge of energy. In many places there are processions, dances and celebrations, often involving bonfires and special costumes. Different areas of the country have their own May Day customs, from 'Crowning the May Queen' to Maypole dances. Originally a tall pole, often a ship's mast, was put up in the village square, garlanded with flowers and topped with long coloured ribbons. Young dancers wove in and out round the pole to folk music, creating webs or a striped pattern. This could be interpreted as bringing together the fertilizing energy of the sky to the receptive and nurturing Earth. Famous hobby horse dances still take place in Padstow, Cornwall, soon followed by the Helston village Furry Dance through flower-decked streets.

Warm weather and longer days in May mark the start of the Summer season, the flourishing of plants and the promise of the first naturally grown fruits. Nature needs human partnerships to overcome the harm we have done to the planet and the biosphere. Working in a garden or an allotment, or even tending a window box or a potted herb, can be very rewarding. It allows time for thought, for slowing down and being out under the sky. Lawns don't have to be cut every week, nor do they have to be just grass. Wild flowers can be beautiful, even if only in a small patch or forgotten corner. Bees and insects will benefit from a bit of grass neglect.

Gardening is not difficult, although some of the experts on television make it seem so. Nurseries want to sell you more tools, lots of different short-lived plants and garden chemicals. Nearly all of these are unnecessary. If you want to learn about successful gardening, or gather some new flowers for your plot, go and ask a neighbour. If things grow in their soil they will do so in yours and most gardeners will share knowledge, and seedlings or cuttings too. They often lend tools and personal hands-on expertise. Dare to ask – it is a magical process.

Value Your 'Weeds'

Weeds are not always harmful as many used to be eaten – dandelions in salads, teas made from cleavers and wild mint, and medicinal tinctures and balms from marigolds and comfrey. Places where Nature can flourish are not tidy and neat, with spaced out flowers on bare earth, they are scrambles of tall and short plants, fruiting bushes and trees. Where there is space, something else will grow, be it ground cover like sweet woodruff, or campanulas, daisies, forget-

me-nots and red and white clover. Depending on the local soil and
weather conditions, a wide variety of vegetation will flourish. Many
wild plants as well as those in gardens, offer valuable nectar and
pollen for bees, who in turn fertilize fruits and create honey. Every
single growing thing has some use, even if it is pulled up and turned
into next year's compost!

Only by getting to know plant life, from the humblest weed to
the most glorious flower, can we identify with these vital species,
not only delighting in how they affect our normal senses but also
realizing how they influence our spiritual wellbeing. Being among
green growing things offers a calm place and mental space for intro-
spection. Because imagination and focused mindfulness are powerful magical tools, here is an exercise which may bring positivity and
creative thinking.

Grow Your Inner Plant

Choose a time when you won't be interrupted for about ten minutes, shut off distractions and sit comfortably upright. Look at a
seed or nut, or visualize what one looks like, and close your eyes.
Take a few deep, slow breaths in and out and allow yourself to relax
and concentrate on that seed. Feel as if you are safely enclosed in a
protective shell into which only helpful ideas can seep. For a few
moments, hold that sense of potential. Imagine as strongly as you
can that you are that seed, enwrapped in gentle earth which will
allow you to grow. Within you you may feel the desire to expand
and send forth a first tender shoot, up towards the light. Become
aware of light and air around you. Reach up, strengthening and
expanding into a young seedling. Imagine time passing.

Your magical self-plant will put out more leaves and develop a
stem. You may become aware of expansion and new experiences.
Take your time, savouring each inner moment, but remain focussed
on 'being a plant'. Sense the passing of days and nights, of light and
darkness, the seasons from Spring into Summer, and of reaching
upwards. You may realize what sort of plant or herb you have connected with. Allow flower buds to form. Your stem may be caressed

by a breeze, your imaginary leaves may be showered with rain drops. All the time you are maturing. Sense the flowers opening and being visited by pollinating insects. Perhaps you will smell the petals and hear bees buzzing. Remain calm as they are harmless to you, and your nectar and pollen benefit them.

Now a fruit containing new seeds is forming, wrapped in a green pod but gradually ripening as the year magically passes you by. Soon the seeds will be released to fall to earth, or be carried by the wind. Then they are enfolded in the fertile ground and your task has been completed.

Let the sense of being a plant fade away, become more aware of your body on the chair, your feet on the floor, your breathing and the things around you. Open your eyes and remain still until you feel properly grounded in yourself. It is often a good idea to write down your experiences, even if on a first attempt nothing much seems to have happened. You might be stepping into a new dimension of inner experience which can have quite profound effects, not always immediately. Try this or a similar journey into the imagination as it is the basis of constructive magic, and a skill well worth mastering, with patience and perseverance.

If you find it hard to imagine this series of images you could act it out, from a curled position, even if in a chair, to sending out a limb, uncurling your fingers from a loose fist, stretching upwards, perhaps miming the opening flower with its spreading petals. You could try holding something to represent a fruit in your cupped hands and then gently releasing it like a falling seed. Be imaginative and creative in this and the other exercises in this book. You could turn the 'Growing plant' into a dance, or get children or friends to enact it with you. The possibilities are endless. All of them will give you a closer connection to Nature and other realms of creation, which can have surprising effects.

11

SUMMER, THE BLOSSOMING OF THE HUMAN SOUL

The Summer months are an ideal time for you, your family and friends to get out of doors. Many modern people who spend a lot of time indoors miss out on the actual physical and mental benefits from being out in the open air. Many are deficient in Vitamin D, the sunshine vitamin which can be absorbed through the skin even if it isn't sunny. Our bodies cannot store this vitamin, so regular doses of the great outdoors can be important for our wellbeing, and especially for our children. From a young age exposure to fresh air, room to run about and play with friends is essential for everyone's health. Walking briskly is a good form of exercise that doesn't cost anything except time and commitment. Paying to go into a gym, breathing recirculated air and becoming hot and tired don't always have the same advantages, in the long run. Experiencing the stimulation of the mind, spirit and body when strolling through a garden to enjoy the flowers, or being out with fresh air touching your skin is truly life-enhancing.

Trying Gentle Exercises
Gentle movement keeps you fit and ensures that your joints and tendons work well, whatever your age. Some people enjoy exercise

with instructors in Pilates, Yoga or T'ai Chi. Each of these works on the body's core strength, balance, breathing and calmness. There are all sorts of classes to share, as well as instruction and demonstrations on You Tube, for example. As well as physical movements, learning to be still, silent and inward-looking can bring mental and spiritual peace and illumination. There are dozens of different techniques, but it is important to enjoy whatever you choose. Often results are not immediate, which can be disappointing, but a few weeks or months of working at a particular exercise or skill will pay off in the long run. Some places offer holidays which combine exercise regimes with vegetarian or vegan diets, massage, spa treatments and relaxation and meditation classes.

In the long days of June and the warm days of July, as well as stretching your physical muscles, it is a good opportunity to sit in a garden and become aware of the flying things that you might see.

There are familiar birds which you can tempt into your garden by offering grains and meal worms, leaving areas of dug earth so they can forage, and letting some flowers go to seed too. The stillness and patience of meditation often allows wild creatures to come close, so don't be surprised if birds alight near you, or sing from your fence or roof. It is the smaller creatures that you might like to pay attention to, the various bugs and bees, the butterflies, moths and sometimes, at eventide, bats.

The Butterflies and the Bees

Many people dislike insects as some do bite, like mosquitoes, but bees and wasps only sting if you attack them, flap about or tread on them barefoot. There are lots of insects that are seen as pests, but even wasps are beneficial to us as they eat aphids. They also make extraordinary paper nests out of chewed wood pulp, and fortunately aren't usually around for very long. Hornets do sting and are bigger than wasps, and some varieties of hornets destroy honey bees in their hives. Honey bee workers, which are the females that gather the pollen and nectar for honey, can be quite pale, or gingery or almost black with paler stripes in colour.

There are also lots of species of bumble bees. Unlike honey bees, most bumbles live in much smaller colonies, or are solitary. They love the nectar and pollen of flowers like foxgloves, cotoneasters and geraniums, and in gardens will nibble their way into the back of the flowers of aquilegias. Their furry, un-aerodynamic bodies humming in the lavender bushes, or flying around in evening twilight, are well worth watching. Bumbles are mostly black with yellow, red, buff or white stripes or tail ends. Some are quite small whilst others look really big, especially when the 'queens' are about. Bees of all sorts are fascinating and many of our food plants depend on them to be fertilized. You can often meet beekeepers at County Shows, as collecting and selling honey is a growing hobby. Even in cities there are productive hives and the urban bees have many gardens with a wide variety of flowers to forage in, whereas country hives may only have oilseed rape or flax to gather nectar from. The honey from these varied sources is quite different.

Other beautiful flying insects include beetles, like glittering green rose chafers, ladybirds, butterflies, moths and dragonflies. Each of these tiny and mostly beneficial creatures has a fascinating life cycle. Some moths are extraordinary colours, like pink elephant hawk moths or privet hawk moths whose bright green caterpillars are as long as a human little finger. Others show red or orange on their wings like garden tiger moths or burnet moths.

Of course butterflies are brighter still – red admirals, peacock butterflies, yellow brimstones and painted ladies, which sometimes arrive in large numbers.

Useful Sources of Information
There are lots of excellent books published by Collins, who have issued pocket-sized guides to butterflies, wild flowers, trees and fungi. These little books are handy to carry around to help anyone identify what they are seeing. Our ancestors would have held a lot of this sort of information in their heads, as the arrival of certain creatures would indicate fine weather, or be omens of things to come. It is another vast area of awareness of the natural world and its spiritual significance. As it is around us all the time, we do owe Nature a lot of care. Some garden insects can afflict us, like blackfly, while others attract us, including many butterflies. We should be careful with garden chemicals as they may poison slugs, but also harm hedgehogs and thrushes. Use organic treatments wherever possible.

The Summer Solstice
Midsummer brings the longest days, which were of great importance to our ancestors. Many of the ancient stone circles, mounds and earthworks were aligned to the Solstices at Midsummer and Midwinter. These must have been times of gathering, rituals, celebrations and magic. People may have come together to exchange ideas, seek healing and meet up with kindred. Livestock might have

be bartered and feasting seems to have taken place, according to recent archaeological discoveries. Even today groups of Pagans and several Druid orders meet at ancient sacred sites like Stonehenge, Avebury, Stanton Drew and Glastonbury, for example. Some welcome the rising sun at Midsummer, or the setting sun at Midwinter. These are times of light, of worldly experiences, connecting to the balance point in the solar year. You might want to make these special in your own way, with parties or ritual, gathering friends and family to acknowledge the height of the season.

Lammas or 'Loaf-Mass'

Later in the farming calendar, the Feast of Lammas, at the beginning of August, was of great importance. This was harvest time when wheat and barley were, and still are, reaped to provide food and drink through the Winter. Corn was needed for bread, barley for beer, and many other field crops like flax for seeds and linen were gathered in and stored carefully. Now oilseed rape and maize form an essential source of sustenance, as well as all the crops grown in the fields, vegetables, sugar beet, and grass for hay and silage, each garnered in its season. Often each harvest had its own celebrations, dances, feasting, ritualistic plays and religious ceremonies, varying from place to place. Many still do.

Holidays and Pilgrimages

In the Summer many people are able to get away, to the coast or the countryside, or to visit sacred places, which allows them to reconnect with their spiritual side. Pilgrimages were always part of religious practice for many faiths, and whether you adhere to an orthodox religion or consider yourself a Pagan or anything else, some places are really special.

As well as enjoying historic structures and buildings, and different things to eat, you may well discover new wildlife. Summer is a great time for learning about birds, from the common town and garden varieties to the sea birds, and the rarer species of the moors and mountains, and of course those found abroad. There are so many sources of information on identifying our flying feathered friends, and often in protected areas or nature reserves there are viewing hides. These provide printed guides with pictures of the different local species, and frequently experts are on hand to explain what you can see.

Watching wild creatures in their natural habitat is extremely relaxing, as well as being informative. Sometimes in the evening twilight you might see bats, even in cities and near water. The fast flying pipistrelles and horseshoe bats sometimes live in large colonies and in the evening flow out like smoke from their roosts. Local information will tell you where to look, and some bat groups use 'bat detectors', which lower their high pitched calls so humans can hear the squeaks and clicks as they fly overhead, echo-locating their prey. Bats are not harmful and won't get caught in your hair, but watching them chasing moths clustering around a source of light can be a delight.

Holidays by the sea will offer you the opportunity to see coastal birds, gulls and cliff-nesting fulmars, cormorants and puffins in certain places. Watching them skim over the waves or dive for fish, or land on precarious ledges where they nest can offer an exhilarating experience. Over marshland huge flocks of starlings and other birds perform spectacular group flying displays called 'murmurations' at twilight, then suddenly all dive into trees or reeds to roost. Swallows in the sky are seen as a sign of Summer, as are the swifts, which scream as they fly and can catch their insect prey even in cities. As the Summer begins to wane many species of birds migrate south for the Winter, and before they depart may gather in large flocks, on telegraph wires and buildings. Starlings go south, leaving cities in great clouds, but their northern cousins soon also fly south and take their places. The Summer birds have lost their gloss, looking dull speckled-black, but the Winter visitors' feathers shine with a green and purple sheen as well as brighter white starry dots which give them their name.

Learning to Fly – an Exercise in Imagination

If you want to explore the world of flying things you can try another mind exercise. Sit comfortably upright, breathe deeply and slowly for a few minutes and close your eyes. Imagine you are safely wrapped in a warm, protective shell. Become aware of a feeling of enclosure and notice a crack of light. You want to reach out, spread yourself towards it. You sense freedom, but you also feel safe. You find yourself in a nest, watched over by a parent bird. You are cared for, and quickly grow, from a small ball of fluff into a strong fledgeling. You stretch your wings and legs, bask in warm sunlight, enjoy the breeze. Days and nights pass, and the impulse to fly gets stronger. You instinctively want to soar on the wind, but at first can only flap and jump.

One day the wind catches your outspread wings and you take off, knowing somehow to control the feathers that help you stay airborne, learning to steer clear of obstacles, seeing the world around you from a new, higher perspective. You feel free but secure, trusting your wings and feathers to keep you aloft, navigating a new element. After a while of this enjoyment, you are drawn back to a cosy nest, welcomed by your parent birds, nurtured, and allowed to rest.

In the warmth and protection of the nest you allow your bird-self to fade away. You recognize your human form, the firm chair beneath you, and gently return to your usual, relaxed self. Taking a few deep breaths, recall aspects of this flying experience and open your eyes. It is often useful to write down your impressions in your magical diary so that you can look back and see what aspects of your life and inner abilities have progressed.

12

AUTUMN, GATHERING A HARVEST OF WISDOM

When the leaves begin to change colour and all sorts of fruits, both cultivated and wild, are ripening, new aspects of the natural world open up. You might go gathering blackberries for pies and bramble jelly, tasting fresh apples and pears from orchard trees or learning which wild mushrooms are safe to eat. Hazel nuts are falling from their green cups and if you can get to them before the squirrels, they make a tasty and healthy snack. Rose hips and whitethorn haws glow red in the hedgerows, and though fewer people gather these to make preserves or syrup now, they are a wild bounty that can be enjoyed if you learn how. Sloes can be picked to make sloe gin or vodka, and plums will provide sweet fruit for crumbles, wine and jam. Damsons, the small cousins of plums, make exceptional country jam, as do gooseberries, picked when they are really ripe, not the hard, sour green berries found in some shops. There are often 'Pick Your Own' farms where all sorts of fruit can be gathered off the bushes, from the early Summer strawberries and raspberries, black, red and white currants to later crops of cherries and apricots. In some places grapes are grown in huge numbers, to eat in sweet bunches or taken to make wine.

Autumn is a bountiful season when a great variety of fruits and vegetables are available, either from our own gardens or allotments, or from farmers' markets and superstores. Trying new tastes can help you widen your appreciation of health-giving foodstuffs. Autumn is also a time to be grateful. If you think about the effort put in by farmers, fruit-growers and merchants to bring fresh produce to you, a different aspect of Nature will become clear. Not only should you be grateful to the producers but to Mother Nature herself. She provides the soil to grow crops in, her rain and sunshine help bring everything to fruition. If you are able to cultivate a garden with flowers, vegetables and herbs, whether it be a window box, suburban garden or a large tract of land, sowing, nurturing and harvesting produce will benefit you, mind, body and spirit.

Sowing Seeds

The physical effort of preparing land, the mental act of selecting seeds or buying seedlings (plus the physical anticipation of the taste), and the spiritual feelings of accomplishment as you gather a harvest are shown to bring healing and calm. Even when the world is in crisis, turning to gardening, planting a flower border or cultivating herbs for the kitchen or as edible aids to wellbeing can bring enjoyment and relief from stress. Learning about the plant kingdom and its ancient gifts of healing and nourishment might be a completely new field of experience. Show you are grateful by working with Nature instead of flooding your plot with chemicals, tidying every flower bed, and pulling out plants you consider to be weeds. Many of the beneficial insects like bees and butterflies depend on the nectar and pollen from these plants, cultivated and wild ones alike. Try to be in harmony with the times and seasons, the weather and the soil conditions so you can grow things to enjoy, and also share with friends and neighbours. Make compost if you have room. Recycle plant waste, twigs and spent flower heads as these can fertilize the earth, or feed small creatures and birds.

A List of Gratitude

An exercise you can try at this time of harvest is to write a list of all the things you are grateful for. This can be material things like home, occupation, relationships, family, friends and treasured possessions. But it can also be for ephemeral things, experiences, feelings and discoveries. Every person has their own special list, and it is best to keep it to yourself. Certainly some aspects of life will not have gone as well as expected or plans will have failed to materialize. It is easy to feel disappointed or let down, or become angry and upset in some situations. You may have been frightened or challenged, lied to or overlooked.

It is likely that you yourself have been unkind on occasion or have let people down, failed to keep promises and done things that you aren't proud of. When you are trying to develop spiritual wellbeing, it is important that you are able to acknowledge your own faults and failings, but that you are not held down by them. Time passes and it helps to have a positive attitude to the past. Being weighed down with regret or guilt will not aid your mental or spiritual health.

Try to find ways of looking forward to a brighter future and a healthier and better balanced life path. It is hard to make this happen but if you are able to think positively and maintain a balanced position in the world you live in, you will feel better. Knowing about the natural world in all its aspects, being able to relate to the basic elements, to the tides and seasons, the plants and animals can give you a secure structure to move forward. Giving thanks, being generous, not only with cash but also with time spent helping others can be rewarding. Being quiet, listening to your body so you can deal with any situation that bothers you, learning to be 'mindful', to meditate and to be still are not wastes of time, but arts that strengthen, calm and fulfil your life. It is said that the more you give, the more you will receive; not in material terms generally, but as happiness and contentment. Being aware of what is around you will bring knowledge and wisdom, neither of which can be bought.

Revealing the Hidden

Autumn can be a time of revelation. As the leaves fall and the branches show their forms as dark skeletons against the sky, imagine how you could feel if all your worries and outworn ideas fell away. This can be a time of letting go, of reorganizing and downsizing. There are probably a number of areas in your home, your life and your thoughts which could do with re-examination. The thing about spiritual awakening or re-awakening is that it can open up new perspectives. Although a lot of inner focus can look like selfishness or self-centredness, if you are not willing to value yourself, be honest about your lifestyle, health or problems, then who else is? Self-assessment can be an important tool, but it needs to be private. The traditional way of doing this was in a 'magical diary', a physical book into which you write, by hand, your hopes and fears, your successes and failures openly. Perhaps you could divide a page down the middle and put positives on one side and negatives on the other. This can be a deep, emotional, but cathartic process. It can also lead to release and a feeling to being set free.

The Autumn Equinox around 21 September is a time of balance again, when day and night are equal in length. The Sun enters the Sign of Libra, the Scales on which, in mythology, the soul of an individual was weighed after death. The ancient Egyptians believed in an elaborate afterlife ritual, recorded on the walls of their tombs and on papyrus. It was thought that the soul could be weighed against the Feather of Ma'at, the Goddess of Truth and Justice. A whole series of ethical questions were posed to the spirit of the dead person to which the answer was expected to be 'No!'. These questions included such concepts as theft from a holy place, murder, betrayal and cruelty. There was one last question which was different and that was 'Will anyone weep at your passing?'. These are things to think about in your own life, and maybe write down in your magical book.

Gathering in

Harvest in the fields was traditionally a time of reckoning as it would mean the difference between a Winter of plenty and one of starvation. Usually this began around Lammas in August. This name Lammas comes from Anglo-Saxon for 'Loaf-mass'. Folk were far more reliant on their corn, root crops and fruit than we are, who have freezers to preserve food and planes to bring us in strawberries at Christmas. Most of us have too much food and seldom even feel hungry, but this is a fairly new state of affairs. Failed harvests, drought, floods, wars and wildfires still trouble large parts of the world. Only by living within our means and not squandering resources or plundering other nations' foodstuffs can each of us contribute to the solution of these worldwide problems. It is necessary to understand where the things we eat or use come from and at what cost to the people who supply them. Although much of this is bought with money, it does not replace the valuable materials or farm produce. They can't eat pound coins or dollar bills.

There used to be all sorts of Harvest Home customs to celebrate the local produce, from the Cornish 'Crying the Neck' in the corn fields when the last standing wheat was ritually cut and carried to the barn. Stalks were and still are cut and woven into corn dollies and other lucky shapes to keep the spirit of the harvest safe until the next sowing. Many areas had their individual magical shapes, from female figures to horseshoes and cornucopias. All traditions seems to have preserved some of the ears of wheat or barley, and the dried grains would be added to next year's seed corn. This was considered to add to the fertility and health of the new crop. It also united the farming communities and gave thanks to their hard work. Harvest suppers were often held, sharing the autumnal bounty of fruit and bread, cheese and cider.

The gathering of apples, pears, plums, sloes, elderberries and blackberries provided a taste of sweetness and the prospects of ciders, perry and fruit wines for the Winter to come. Herbs were gathered and dried for flavouring and medicine through the cold time, and all kinds of pickles, jams and preserves were made. Many of these are still important parts of people's diets, especially homemade ones. Most of these culinary arts are simple, although they can be time-consuming; they are, however very life affirming and meditative. Stirring a simmering pan of chutney or bramble jelly, pouring the colourful mixture into hot jars and delighting in the finished product is a personal harvest to savour. Even if you don't grow your own fruit, some can be gathered from the wild or bought from farmers' markets. Home-made produce, created with love and care can make useful gifts, and a way of sharing Nature's bounty with your friends and family.

Remembrance

As October rolls on, the leaves fall and colder weather sets in. The first frost often occurs at this time, and livestock would be brought in to Winter quarters. Some would be culled and salted or smoked to preserve the meat for the icy lean months ahead. Because there would be things that had to be used up quickly, this became a time of gathering and sharing food and drink. Originally it was a time of remembering the dead at All Hallows' Eve, when it was thought that ghosts would be abroad, and other eerie happenings might occur. There was a custom in Scotland of 'guising', turning clothes inside out, masking faces with ashes and playing tricks on unpleasant neighbours. The disguises were so that any nasty spirits would not be able to recognize people to harm them, neither would the neighbours who had found their cattle missing or their gates taken off the hinges know who to blame. This custom gradually evolved into the partying and fancy dress more commonly known as 'Trick or Treating' today. Children enjoy dressing up as witches and wizards, ghosts and vampires, and sometimes comic book heroes and going from house to house asking for sweets.

Originally they would perform a 'trick', perhaps a song or dance, or recite a poem, and if no treat was forthcoming they would play a joke on the people. In narrow streets children used to tie door-knockers on opposite houses together so folk couldn't get out or throw rotten fruit at their windows. The plastic cauldrons and fake broomsticks and all the garish sweets, masks and bloody costumes have evolved from this solemn time of remembering the dead into a brash extravaganza, often in really bad taste. It now has nothing to do with the end of all the harvests and preparing for Winter, and simple country customs, probably from Scotland, of disguise and rural revenge, having migrated to America, have literally returned to haunt us!

Samhain

Hallowe'en was once called 'Samhain', the end of Summer and modern Pagans see it as an important festival, along with Beltane in May, Lammas in August and Imbolc in February. Rituals are performed by some witch covens or groves of Druids to honour their ancestors or the founders of their tradition. It is a time for reflection and remembrance of those who have gone before, sharing their wisdom and knowledge. It can be a time for reminiscences, story telling and sharing of recollections. Maybe people still sit around a hearth and talk about childhood and relatives only occasionally seen at Christmas or birthdays. Speaking about grandparents and where they lived, recalling visits or adventures from long ago, holidays and activities enriches those special moments. Of course, not everyone

has happy memories; times might have been hard, family members unfeeling or holidays unthinkable. Sometimes looking back it is possible to understand situations which seemed so cruel at the time, and see them in the light of later experience. Some of these ideas might form the basis for meditation at this time of year.

The end of October and the beginning of November have various activities associated with death – from the death of Summer and the beheaded corn of harvest to the spooky rites of Hallowe'en, through to Bonfire Night, which commemorates the execution of the conspirator Guy Fawkes, who was planning to murder King James I. It is also the time of Remembrance Sunday around 11 November, which marked the end of World War I, one of the greatest losses of life in Europe. The Cenotaph was put up as a focus, and this 'empty tomb' in Whitehall, London is where representatives of the Armed Services, Parliament, the Royal Family and leaders of many faiths pay their respects and lay wreaths in honour of the fallen. This is a solemn procession accompanied by emotional and funereal music from military bands. If you witness it, it is hard not to be touched, nor to forget the countless men and women who have died in conflicts around the world. Perhaps some of your relatives were among them.

Funeral Feelings

In recent times so many people have experienced loss, and during the Covid pandemic the traditional rites concerning last days' care, funeral ceremonies and gatherings for wakes or memorial services were banned. No one can really prepare for the death of someone close to them and during this time the vital support of family and friends had been denied. Too many patients were isolated from their family, cared for by strangers, forbidden to touch or hug during those unredeemable hours. The experience of grief is not always immediate, especially in an unfamiliar situation, as often there is too much bureaucracy to deal with. We do not learn how to deal with loss and the emotions it brings. Feelings of anger, of deep sadness, of abandonment and alone-ness can sweep over anyone at unexpected times and without physical support these emotions are exaggerated.

People are embarrassed to show emotions and don't like bursting into tears in public. Yet this is a natural experience. Not only do some people feel uncomfortable expressing their inner feelings, but those they come into contact with are made to feel awkward too. Knowing what to say to a bereaved person is a difficult thing to do. Should you even mention the one they have lost? Should you be chatty and up-beat or solemn and mournful? Often the questions they most want to hear is 'But how are you?' or 'What can I do to help?'.

Talking about shared memories can often be comforting, recalling happier times when the lost loved one was there. Each situation at each gathering of friends or family has to be judged individually. Can a joke be appropriate or would that be seen as disrespectful? Often those touches and hugs that were forbidden during the pandemic can be the kindest approach. No one is really forgotten and a time will come when it is all right to talk about them.

It can be a spiritual blow too, and thoughts like 'How could God do this to me? How could Fate snatch away such a good person in the midst of their life?' can cause a loss of faith. The realization that love, no matter how strong, cannot save someone can be a crushing experience. Dying creates a lot of problems, many of which involve not only family and friends, but legal advisors, medical people and funeral directors.

When anyone dies there are bound to be all sorts of folk who need or want to be involved. Funerals used to be extensive and elaborate affairs, with 'wakes' and burial services or gatherings at a crematorium. There would be special traditionally black clothes, and a procession from a church to the cemetery. Religious prayers and ritual customs accompanied the interment. Some faiths expect to bury their dead within twenty-four hours, but under pandemic restrictions and with large numbers of deceased to deal with, this was not possible. All these things brought added distress, as well as the financial arrangements, disposing of the effects of the person who had died, reading their will and acting according to their last wishes. It must have been a dreadful experience for so many families. Even the planning of a memorial service had to be put on hold as gatherings of more than a handful of people was banned for over a year. This also applied to other group commemorations including weddings and christenings. Choosing the small numbers who were permitted to attend all these important and often once in a life time events presented another problem for the bereaved family. After the funeral or cremation ceremony there was little opportunity to mingle, to hug each other and exchange memories. For some people this pared-back event offered little comfort or support at a time of great spiritual need.

Burial Rites

For some people interment takes place in a woodland burial site or even in a large private garden. Instead of engraved stone memorials, trees or shrubs can be planted, or even wild flowers sown over a meadow where ashes had been scattered. Some wildlife charities will dedicate a tree or patch of woodland to act as a memorial, perhaps with a small name and date plaque to commemorate the deceased. So many different methods of laying our loved ones to rest are now possible, allowing people to remember and reminisce at a later date. A new way of death and interment evolved now the huge Victorian cemeteries with their elaborate marble statues have filled up or become overgrown. These old cemeteries have gained a new lease of life as wildlife havens, and trees have grown up among the graves. They can be very peaceful, even in cities, where it is possible to sit and contemplate the mysteries of life and death.

Most religions have ideas about the afterlife, some teaching that a good, ethical and kind existence will be rewarded in heaven or paradise, whereas sinners will be punished by eternal damnation. Other faiths suggest that after the end of one human existence, the soul is reborn through reincarnation, to live as a person who has opportunities to benefit from previous good deeds or make up for errors. Some individuals believe that when you die that is the end of everything, and that you have no eternal spirit to be reborn. Others feel that each human soul is absorbed into the one creative Spirit, becoming part of a universal afterlife form. Each of these ideas should form the basis of deep and personal contemplation. We can't know for certain what happens after death, but there is quite a lot of information about young children 'remembering' that they have lived somewhere else, and had different parents or relatives. There are techniques of 'past life recall' which, under the guidance of an ethical and practised guide, can allow such recollections to be awakened. Not everyone was Cleopatra or Napoleon! Many who do have past life memories, often received in dreams or through directed meditation, recall being unexceptional folk, country dwellers with rustic trades, traditional skills and ordinary homelife. These memories may be as recent as a world war or as long ago as ancient Egypt, Greece or in the Far East, and the memories can be really clear and historically correct.

A Memories Box

A practical activity you might like to consider is the creation of a 'keepsake caddy', a box or tin into which actual artefacts can be stored. Many people now keep their photos on their phones or laptops, but in the past photos were actual pictures, stored in albums or cardboard boxes. These could be brought out at family gatherings to show to younger members of the clan, and recall the events they depict. Each fading image would have a part of a story to tell, in black and white or in colour. Today pictures captured digitally on a phone are seldom printed, nor even shared at a later date.

To make a memory box can be a useful way of reinventing the albums of the past. Ideally a nice container can form the basis of this collection and all manner of small things, souvenirs as well as pictures, can be stored. Like the magical diary, this can be a private project where very personal mementoes are gathered together. If you start to look around you may be surprised what you can find from times past that is still meaningful to you. Each may bring a smile or even a tear. The objects we keep usually have mental and spiritual links to people or places, and it can be a purifying process revisiting some aspects of the past. Experiencing painful or joyous emotions are deep ways of connecting to our spiritual being.

Perhaps actually making a wooden box, or creating an artistic design to cover a strong cardboard container can be the first step in this remembrance process. Charity shops or craft fairs often sell beautiful boxes, and searching for a suitable 'keepsake caddy' at home or elsewhere can be a voyage of discovery in its own right. No one should dictate what you choose, or what you put in it, neither should this be a one-off occasion on a wet Winter evening. It is a way of building up and preserving memories, touching things, looking and really seeing old pictures and the places and people they show.

You might prefer to share this task with family members, or encourage a younger relative to make his or her memory box. It may not seem important to keep hand-drawn pictures, old letters, post-cards from distant places or holiday souvenirs when you are young, but later in life you might come to treasure these items, and the memories they hold. Often small, trivial objects or gifts have a deep meaning and special connections to their owner, although they are looked on as junk by anyone else.

They can be used as subjects for meditations. Sit quietly, breathe deeply and relax and then focus on a single item. Look at it, feel it, sense anything you can and then close your eyes and see what comes. If you stay relaxed and mentally poised, you will get impressions, pictures, feelings, even scents, somehow connected with the object. Learn what it means to you, to your mind, body and spirit. Like most magical activities it can take a while to learn, being able to switch on a different kind of sensitivity, or switch it off when in more mundane settings.

13

WINTER, VALUING WITHDRAWAL, REST AND RECONSIDERATION

Winter may seem like a time of withdrawal as cold, wet or icy weather does not encourage us to go outdoors so much; as daylight hours are short, we tend to turn inward. However, clear skies and occasional warmer spells may still allow us all to reconnect with the stars, and with the trees by night and day. It can be depressing and in the past was often a lean time of year, especially if harvests had been poor and livestock sickly. Between Midwinter and mid-February was called 'the hungry gap' or 'the Dismal' as nothing much was growing and stored grain and preserved meat were not very nourishing. However, as soon as the days began to lengthen, people were a bit more hopeful about the future. This is why there are so many celebrations in late December all round the world, leading up to the calendar New Year. Because very little work on farms could be done in the short, wet or frosty days, everyone could meet up and share whatever was left. This is why cakes with preserved fruit, or fat cattle or poultry were eaten, so they didn't need to be fed any more. In a time of famine there was feasting, and in a dismal month there would be gatherings and happiness.

Yuletide Customs

One of the tasks many people do at this time of year, in preparation for Christmas or Yuletide, is to look at lists of friends and relatives they need to send messages or even gifts to at the coming festival. Often this can be a heart-warming process, but it can also be sad when we find out that some valued people have died, or that we have lost touch with them. The tradition of sending actual cards is not very old, beginning when it became cheap to print pictures around 1850, and send them out by post around the world. The Victorians created elaborate designs, some hand-coloured or decorated with lace, each a special message to loved ones. Today an e-mail does not have the same impact, and some of us keep old cards or letters for the memories they bring.

Re-examining our contact lists can give us a sense of our position in the world. If we are fortunate enough to have lots of dear friends and close relatives, we can count ourselves lucky. But sadly many people feel very lonely, and the bright lights, decorations and gift-giving leaves them down-hearted. It can be an opportunity to reach out to those less fortunate than ourselves. Charities are always looking for volunteers, in their shops or at food banks, or at the special meals they arrange around Midwinter. You may not feel able to participate in these activities, but perhaps you can find spare clothes, bedding or other useful items that can be donated to help the homeless.

Sometimes people might have been forced to move out due to house fires, or storm damage, flood or gales. No one can tell when Nature will destroy the very foundation of our existence, and anyone can find themselves in need. Charity in any form is often uplifting to both mind and spirit. Random acts of kindness may have far-reaching and beneficial effects. Giving produce or flowers from your garden can bring a smile to a neighbour, or help a poorly friend recover sooner. Often working at a charity event or sharing something can lead to new friendships being formed. Even befriending a lonely older person, or even finding ways to help children with reading or learning about wildlife and Nature can benefit everyone involved. Everyone needs friends and companions to go for walks or share simple outings or adventures with.

The Mind Power of Poetry and Music

Winter may make us spend more time indoors, but it can be an opportunity to learn a new skill or finish a handicraft hobby. Research shows that doing crosswords or sudoku number puzzles helps keep the brain working. Some of these may seem quite challenging to begin with, but gradually you master the cryptic clues or the patterns of numbers in the grid and this leads to a positive sense of satisfaction and achievement. Jigsaws are another pastime which can help some folk feel calm and relaxed. Maybe you can share your puzzles with the neighbour, or learn from an acquaintance how to solve more testing crosswords. No skill, no matter how simple seeming, is a waste of time. Even reviving the arts of actual letter writing, calligraphy or creating poetry or short stories can be extremely pleasurable. Often the idea of writing a story or tackling haiku verses can appear much harder than it is.

Haikus are poems
with five then seven then five
syllables in them.

That statement, divided into three lines is a haiku.

A flower opens.
And turns its face to the Sun.
Spring has arrived.

This Japanese form of poetry often describes things in Nature, the seasons, the weather and human relationships in such a concise way that it connects with emotion or inner spirit. There are lots of sources of all kinds of poetry, both classical and modern, rhyming and blank verse, short heartfelt pieces and long verse epics. All are worth exploring as they can help with feelings of loss or joy or loneliness. Children used to learn poetry at school and even in later life can recite the ones they remembered from their childhoods. It can help too on sleepless nights, working through a verse recalled from the past.

Limericks are another simple form of poetry, often humorous, that can be tried.

There was a faith healer from Deal,
Who said 'Although pain isn't real,
If I sit on a pin, and it punctures my skin,
I dislike what I fancy I feel!'

is such a limerick. Do have a go – you might surprise yourself.

Poetry of all sorts speaks to a different part of your mind than plain text. It can bring forth tears or laughter, and may evoke a deep, heartfelt emotion that has no other expression. Poetry can also be shared, read out and enjoyed by friends or family. It can be a comfort at funerals or simply be uplifting in times of stress. Today there are countless ways to find poetry – in books or in the words of songs, and at Midwinter, in Christmas carols which tell a story, evoke emotions and can cheer people up. Carols were originally dances for celebrations at any time of year, as are the large number of folk songs. Many of these are concerned with love, with loss or with rural seasonal activities. Joining a choir is another way of making friends and most places have choirs of all sorts and abilities, not only connected with churches. Some are inclined to classical music, or songs from shows, or popular music. No matter what your voice is like there could be opportunities to join and learn how to stay in tune and blend your voice with the others. Playing a musical instrument is another important skill to benefit mind and spirit. Music, poetry, theatre and dance all touch the souls of those who create them and of those who participate in them and those who hear or witness them. Don't under-estimate the value of music as a spiritual tonic, whatever your personal taste and way of hearing it.

Midwinter Celebrations

Traditionally Midwinter was marked in a number of different ways, some based on established religions but others more concerned with the Solstice which brings the shortest day and longest night. Druid groves and Pagans may celebrate the Solstice, when the Sun seems to stand still in the sky, by acknowledging the dark. If indoors some groups will put out every light and sit to meditate in darkness. Then using a flint and steel rather than a match a new flame is kindled to light a candle. This light may be shared to other lamps or nightlights around a circle.

Christmas too is a festival of light when the promised Child of Light, the Star Child, is born in the dark stable according to the Christian story. Several other faiths have a divine infant arriving around the middle of Winter and these mystic 'birthdays' occur a few days after the Winter Solstice, on 25 December when it is just possible to see that the day is getting a little bit longer. Mithras, the hero of a pre-Christian Roman military religion, was born in a cave on that day and was considered to be a saviour of mankind, and the ancient Egyptians worshipped Horus the magical son of Isis and Osiris at this time.

A Midwinter Rite

Here is a simple ritual and words, which may be shared if there are several participants. The Lighter of the First Flame kindles their candle and says, 'I am the Light.' They turn to their neighbour and say, 'I give you the Light.' As that person takes the candle they say, 'You are the Light.' Then the recipient and the lighter say, 'We are the Light,' and the recipient repeats this so the candle is passed round the circle, with everyone joining in saying, 'We are the Light'. A nightlight in a safe holder may be used or a lit taper might be used to ignite each individual's lamp. You can even use a switched on electric torch for safety! This very simple ritual can have profound emotional and spiritual effects as the flame grows from a single point to an illuminated circle.

The Spiritual Concept of Light

To many faiths, Light is an inspiring concept, promising physical and spiritual illumination. We say 'Light has dawned,' when we understand something or we 'see the Light'. Things that shine, like the Sun, the Moon and the stars have always been of great inner significance. Myths and legends have grown up about these guides to time and space. There are Sun Gods and Goddesses, Moon Goddesses and Gods, and each constellation in the Zodiac has a name and mythic history. Orion, an easily recognized pattern of stars in the Winter sky was seen as a great hunter, followed by Sirius, the dog star, one of the brightest stars in the night sky. The seven stars of the Plough or Arthur's Wain point to the North or Pole star, used in navigation for thousands of years, as it appears to be the central pivot around which the night's stars rotate. Long ago other stars held this vital position.

A star plays a part in the Christmas story, guiding the three Wise Men, who were probably astronomers, to the place where Jesus and his family were lodging. This was a sacred pilgrimage for them, to bring symbolic gifts to the Holy Child. Two of these traditional offerings were precious incenses, frankincense and myrrh, both derived from bushes, and gold from the Earth herself. Today it is the expectation of presents and parties, sparkling decorations and an illuminated tree that many young folk look forward to, rather than carol singing, religious services and visiting older relatives. The birth of a Redeemer and a promise of eternal life is no longer a lure. The brightly-lit shops, the tinsel and pretty wrapping paper and the gifts they contain, the delicious Christmas dinner and all that goes with it are so enchanting. Decorated wreaths on doors and the Christmas tree with its coloured lights and glittering baubles all deflect people's thoughts from the original simple message of hope, and Christmas has become a festival of materialism and gluttony. A few green branches, a good dinner and gathering the family around the fire to exchange news used to be enough.

Traditional Yuletide Symbols

Many of the symbols, including the Yule log, now chocolate cake rather than an oak tree trunk set to burn on an open hearthfire throughout the festival, and the greenery of holly, ivy and mistletoe all have their roots in ancient Yuletide traditions. These are mementoes of Mother Nature grafted onto a newer celebration. Yule, the feast of the turning wheel from Winter towards Spring, was significant to our ancestors who timed important activities in their lives by the position of the Sun on the horizon. This is why many ancient megalithic structures like Stonehenge and Avebury have markers placed to indicate the rising or setting Sun at the Solstices or Equinoxes. The relationship between the Earth and the sky had to be renewed at different times of the year, marked by the setting Sun or Moon or significant stars. This spiritual interaction supported the seasons, the pattern of agricultures and animal husbandry. Now we all get time from clocks and not the sky, and sow seeds in the month it says on the packet! We are out of step with the cosmos, and it can be upsetting on an inner level.

Santa Claus or Father Christmas, with his reindeer-drawn sleigh, red and white costume and a big sack, brings presents for children who have been good. In some countries those children who had been bad were threatened with being put in a sack and taken away. Father Christmas had to be provided with food and drink in the hearth, the traditional centre of the house, and carrots or apples left out for the reindeer. Some of these customs may come from the tribal Siberian shamans who were said to drink magical potions made from the red and white spotted fly agaric mushroom, which is quite poisonous. This allowed the spirit of the shamans to fly through the air, perhaps accompanied by the reindeer which they herded in the far north. They were healers of the sick and could foretell what was going to happen, but their training was long and hard, a test of spirit and psychic ability, not something that could be learned at a weekend workshop.

Christmas and Nature

Although many aspects of modern Christmas celebrations seem to be wrapped in plastic and tied up with glittery ribbons, at the heart of this Midwinter feast are many connections to Nature too. The Christmas tree was made popular by Queen Victoria's German husband Prince Albert in the late 1800s. On the continent decorated trees with toys, sweets and candles were already part of their Yule celebrations. The gathering of evergreen branches, holly, ivy, mistletoe, laurel and bay to make decorations is much older, as are the carols and songs which list these special plants and trees. Songs include 'Down in Yon Forest', 'The Cherry Tree Carol', 'The Holly and the Ivy', 'King Jesus Hath a Garden' (originally from Holland) and 'Jesus Christ the Apple Tree' (from America), and the song 'On the first day of Christmas my true love gave to me a partridge in a pear tree', which follows up with French Hens, Colley or Calling Birds, and so on. And let's not forget 'Rudolf the Red-nosed Reindeer'! Plants and animals remind us how important they are at this turning point of the year. They have been our spiritual companions since humans first found they could eat them, or use them for medicine.

The earliest symbol of a pub or inn was a bunch of greenery hung over the door. Perhaps this links to the Green Man, the wild spirit of the woods, whose face, though often found in churches, is also carved on lots of old buildings, including inns or taverns. The Green Man seems to signify the enduring spirit of Nature and her annual renewal. This is especially true as Christmas falls three days after the Solstice. It is also a time when angels appear on cards and the top of trees, and are remembered in many songs for playing the part of messengers, which is what angel means.

Not only is greenery a forgotten aspect of the Yuletide celebration, but all sorts of animals have their legendary parts to play, from the donkey Mary rode to Bethlehem and the animals which occupied the stable where Jesus was born. There is a lovely story that if you go into a stable or byre at midnight on Christmas Eve, all the animals will kneel down in honour of this miraculous happening. Of course other characters who get parts in Nativity paintings and plays are the shepherds, watching their flocks of sheep, and probably goats, at night, who kept dogs to scare away wolves or other predators. The three Wise Men or Magi, coming from the East on Epiphany, may have ridden to the stable on camels or horses. Although no one knows for sure what actually happened, or even exactly when, so many parts of the Christmas story retain connections to plants and animals and features of the natural world. Many of these also offer spiritual and emotional impulses too.

Twelfth Night and Mumming Plays

Twelfth Night used to be an important date, now 6 January, when Christmas decorations are taken down and the Yule feasting ends. In earlier times this was Epiphany, when the Wise Men arrived with their gifts. In wealthy households each day between 25 December and 6 January was celebrated with ever more elaborate meals, music, dancing and Mumming Plays. These originally 'mimed' plays enact the battle between St George and a fierce opponent, a Black Knight or even a Dragon. Although St George overcomes all his adversaries, a Doctor character comes in to administer a magical potion. The slain knights are immediately revived and dance away. This is the story of Midwinter when the Dragon of cold is overcome by the healing power of the spring. Though rarer nowadays, there used to be many local versions of this, sometimes performed by members of Morris dancing side, or by school children. The cast often ask for donations and can threaten the audience if they don't make a small payment.

There are other Yule customs where a fee is requested from the carol singers who would go from door to door with lanterns, singing the traditional songs and asking for something from the householders. This could be food and drink like mince pies and beer, or more recently money for a local charity. In South Wales the 'Mari Lwyd', the grey mare, represented by a horse's skull on a pole or costume with snapping jaws, would arrive accompanied by a musician and some dancers. This crew would sing a verse to challenge the householders who were expected to answer back with a witty retort. Both these challenge and answer would get more pointed and rude until one side gave up. The Mari Lwyd and her companions would tease the inmates, snapping at them or the crew would hug the ladies until food and drink was offered. They would then offer a New Year blessing on the house and then depart to threaten a neighbour. These old customs united villagers, allowed them to share whatever was available and brought a bit of fun to a bleak season.

New Year's Days
The first of January brings its own New Year Celebrations, with parties and fireworks. In Scotland First Footers at Hogmanay bring in symbolic tokens of plenty to those who invite them in to join in singing 'Auld Lang Syne' at midnight. For them it is a more important date than 25 December.

There are all sorts of other dates for a New Year tradition. The Chinese New Year is in February when the Moon is new. This marks the transition to both one of the five elements and one of the twelve signs of the Chinese Zodiac, which include animals such as the Rabbit, the Monkey, the Snake and the Rat. In the Western Zodiac, the astronomical New Year begins at the Spring Equinox on 21 March. This date is celebrated by Druids and other Pagans, who see it as a time of rebirth and renewal. Other major faiths have New Year days as well as fasts and feasts throughout the year. You can almost always find some special date to gather with friends, including your own birthday, anniversaries for weddings and the birth of children. These can always be times of reflection as well as for gift-giving and parties. Looking towards your inner life and its landmarks can be a rewarding reconnection between spiritual and mundane life.

PART IV

MAGICAL ARTS – ANCIENT AND MODERN

14

TREES AND THE SPIRIT OF NATURE

With the threat of climate change growing more desperate all the time, the importance of human actions on the natural world has shown us how careless we have been in the past centuries. No one thought that cutting down a forest for wood, or draining a marsh, reshaping a river, mining coal to burn or quarrying would do much harm to the world – now we are becoming too aware that such things in the past have had dire consequences. Some of the changes cannot now be reversed. We cannot recreate the ancient woodlands with all their interlinked wildlife, we cannot drain the reservoirs that flooded villages to provide drinking water. We can't fill in the mines or replace the ore or coal or stone or crystals that were taken away. But we can plant more trees. We can be far more careful in future, taking into account all the possible consequences of any large-scale developments. We might not be able to do this personally as decision-makers, but because we have access to information and have modern ways of asking questions and raising our concerns, we can contribute to the arguments and help seek out solutions.

People have had close relationships with trees for thousands of years, bending their stems to make shelters, burning their wood to keep away predators and cook food. They made tools and weapons from the branches, walking sticks for support, and developed many skills in carving useful implements, food containers, and musical instruments from wood over the centuries. Gradually our ancestors discovered the special properties of each kind of tree. Some reflect its strength or flexibility, or its ability to survive generations as the structure of a home or bridge. Most advances in human history have involved some kind of tree or plant material. In some places special trees have been worshipped, or been seen as symbols of a God or Goddess. They have been seen as way markers on the horizon, spiritual guardians of houses, dwelling places of kindly invisible entities, and suppliers of nourishing fruits. In today's world we do need to rebuild these spiritual connections to Nature, especially with trees because we need each other.

The Qualities of Different Trees

Apple is a tree of magic, called 'the Silver Branch' when it is in flower. The fruit contains a hidden star in the pentagram shape its seeds make when the fruit is cut open cross-wise, and it is a passport to the secret world of faery, allowing entry and, more importantly, return to the waking world. Avalon, the Island of Apples or of the departed in Arthurian legend is also a 'land of dreams', as well as the real place, Glastonbury. And of course you can make cider from the apple's fruit in the Autumn!

Yew symbolizes everlasting life because it is one of the longest-living trees, but its leaves are poisonous. This is one of the reasons yews were planted in sacred places, including churchyards. Some churches are actually younger than the yew trees that grow near them. The graveyards were enclosed with walls or fences to prevent livestock eating the leaves, although many birds relish the deep pink berries. Yews also provided wood for long bows which were so important in medieval battles.

'Y'-shaped dowsing rods were traditionally cut from willow or hazel to help the diviner find water. Wizards always had magical staffs, sorcerers had wands, witches had broomsticks – all instruments for controlling power. Often these were carved from particular trees, which were sacred to the individual practitioner.

They always have to be made by their user. Pine or cypress branches were placed outside houses to indicate a death in Roman times, while medieval taverns had a holly bush outside. Druids honoured oak trees, and would gather mistletoe from rowan, hawthorn or poplar at their Midwinter rites.

To some people, trees are just green blobs on top of brown sticks scattered around the landscape, but to the wise and to those who seek knowledge from Nature they can be great sources of instruction and solace. Each one is unique, in the same way that every person is unique. Even trees grown from seeds of the same parent will differ in size and shape. Some will flourish and be fruitful; others will struggle in any conditions. None of them is perfect! A branch may be crooked, making the shape less symmetrical; some of the leaves may have been nibbled by insects and their Spring flowers may have been spoiled by a hard frost. Each remains a tree, true to itself, and this is a lesson to us all – none of us is perfect, but we can aim to improve. Getting to know trees, in towns and cities, in country and forest, in woodland or alone on a hill is important; every tree has something to teach us about patience and endurance, and the changing seasons. Woodland, whether an orchard, a copse or a forest can be a place for meditation and spiritual renewal. Research has shown that trees communicate through their roots and the chemical signals they give off. They are not single units, but members of a secretly connected community. They can give warnings about insect attack, or share nourishment under the ground if their companions are suffering. Every leaf, twig, branch and trunk will be individual and vary from its neighbours. The chemicals they exude can also be beneficial to people.

Uses of Various Woods

Trees of different species have special properties which our ancestors recognized. Some had great strength, like the mighty oak whose curved timber supported houses or made frames for boats. Ash was used for tool handles, beech for furniture and boards to write on. Its Saxon name is related to the word 'book'. Elm was used to make coffins and for wine barrels, the 'coffin for the vine'. In the days before plastic, each kind of wood was regarded as an important material for thousands of everyday items. Bowls and platters for food and the spoons to eat it with were carved from tree trunks. Boxes, chests, doors and window frames were all made from this resilient material. Hawthorn was used for hedges as it grows very quickly into a thick wall if cut properly. Box wood is very hard and was used for carving chess pieces, and hornbeam, as its robust name suggests, was made into cogs for windmills. Alder wood hardens in water and was used for the soles of clogs and bridge supports; some ancient examples have been dug up in Somerset. Fruit woods, as well as supplying apples and pears, is still used in decorative furniture, as is walnut veneer. Pine trees still provide resin for incense, while birch or maple sap provides a sweet liquor. Once you start to look into this amazing material that grows all over the world, you might be astonished at its variety of specific uses, its beauty and enduring nature.

Healing in Local Woods and Copses

Searching out some trees to aid your own connection with Nature is not difficult. Maps provide keys to green spaces, woodland or forest. Gardens, parks, country estates and town gardens nearly all have trees that you can get close to. They provide shade in Summer, are homes to birds, butterflies and many other small creatures, which are all parts of the web of Nature. Learning to reconnect with trees can be as simple as looking round your home. What is made of wood? How do you feel about trees, and are there any in your garden or street? Trees can do a lot to heal the planet by soaking up carbon dioxide, one of the 'greenhouse gases' that are causing climate change.

Everywhere there are schemes to plant more trees, especially in the Winter when they are dormant. Consider this to be a vital task you might be able to contribute to, even by simply saving acorns or other tree seeds to plant. It is mentally and spiritually rewarding helping other people or charities restore woodland, field hedges or city parks. The feel of a branch in your hand, the smell of the leaves, the beauty of the flowers in Spring, especially of orchards and the nourishing fruit, feed not only our bodies but the spirits within us. In Japan there is a custom called 'Tree Bathing' which is also being encouraged in this country. It is really a simple way of relaxation within any kind of woodland. Take a waterproof blanket and place it in a low branch or under a tree and lie down and relax. Imagine you are bathing in the energy of the trees, allowing deep stillness of body and mind. After about twenty minutes of this you will feel calm and re-energized. Many people are deprived of natural experiences and being in open spaces where you can breathe clean air is very beneficial.

Magical Relationships with Woodland

Different sorts of trees have formed the backbone of a number of magical traditions, each of which can take a lifetime to learn. In the world of the ancient Celtic people, sacred groves were at the heart of their Druidic philosophy. The names of each of the letters of the mystical Ogham or Ogam alphabet were referred to by the Irish name of a tree. A whole system of divination and personal growth could be encapsulated in Ogham writing, and it is still used for charms and amulets.

Another later tree-based magical letter system is that of the Norse Runes. The legend tells how Odin, one of their most important Gods, sacrificed himself to himself by becoming entangled in the branches of a huge ash tree, called Yggdrasil. For nine nights and days he hung there, neither eating nor drinking until he had a revelation. By looking at the shapes of the twigs, how they crossed or branched, he saw sacred writing. When his ordeal ended these were carved on wood and stone and used to create talismans and preserve stories of heroes. Yggdrasil was considered to link the world below the earth with the realm of the sky, so becoming a mighty pillar, up which a magical squirrel called Ratatosk climbed.

The Tree of Life

Many ancient faiths have a concept of a Tree of Life or a Tree of Knowledge. These are depicted in works of art, carvings, and sacred diagrams. One which is an important part of the Western Mystery Tradition is the Qabalistic Tree of Life. This is a glyph, or sacred diagram, which has ten spheres representing the planetary forces, together with angels and powerful concepts, expressed in Hebrew. Connecting the spheres are twenty-two paths which indicate way for a wise person to travel, from Malkuth, the Kingdom of Earth sphere, towards Kether, the Crown, starry pinnacle of achievement. There are countless interpretations of the Tree of Life, and it can take a lifetime of study and meditation to translate this source of wisdom into practical knowledge. Each sphere has a long list of 'correspondences', which include the colour, the angel, the planet, or can be a God or Goddess of one of several pantheons. There are a number of large books that list all these attributions as well as ways to make use in this extensive battery of knowledge in making talismans and special spiritual journeys, called 'Path Working' with magical symbolism. Although mystical and symbolic trees are important aspects of inner work, real living ones are more approachable in modern spiritual terms.

Connecting with Trees

A good way to make an arboreal connection is to do bark or leaf rubbings. Hold a sheet of paper against the tree trunk and with a soft pencil or wax crayon gently rub to produce an imprint of the pattern of the bark, or pick a couple of leaves and lay them on a firm flat surface. Place the paper on top and again gently scribble over them with a pencil. This can produce a beautiful print which can be copied and used as a decoration for cards or letters, for example. Children can enjoy these sorts of activities and it is another way of helping younger folk bond with physical Nature. Experiment with different sorts of leaves or even flowers.

Another way to preserve samples of a tree or plant is to flatten leaves or flowers between two sheets of kitchen paper and then place this 'sandwich' inside a thick book or under a heavy weight. Old printed catalogues are actually useful for this. After a few weeks the flowers will be dry and flat and can be saved in an album. This is a useful skill to master as it is a good way of preserving examples of herbs and medicinal plants, local trees or even flowers from gift bouquets.

If you look on the ground in a wood you may find natural skeletons of the dried leaves which can be quite magical.

A Tree-Bonding Exercise

Ideally you can find a tree to really bond with. You can give it a hug when there is no one you can embrace, and allow yourself to draw on its energy, stability, endurance and natural beauty. A very simple exercise in tree power is to stand with your back supported by the trunk and close your eyes. Imagine an earthy energy flowing like honey up the trunk of the tree, from its roots deeply clasped in the ground up towards its branches, twigs and leaves. Feel this upward surge through the wood and also through your own being. Imagine it nourishing you with spiritual food, drawn from the heart of the Earth, filling you with strength and calmness. Put aside any feelings of embarrassment or foolishness and concentrate on that up-flowing power. Once you have absorbed the slow moving honey-like energy from below, consider the sky fall of sun light upon the leaves.

This is a golden feeling, like the brilliant sparkles of fireworks or bubbles in a fizzy drink. These trickle downwards, through the leaves and twigs and branches, into the trunk and down through the roots to the Earth. It can also be sensed passing down your body. It brings light and solar energy, sparkling through each part of you, refreshing and energizing you. Absorb this sensation for a little while. Finally see if you can sense both flows, the upward steady surge of dark golden Earth power and the down-rushing energy of sunlight and twinkling starlight all through you, from head to feet, from fingers to toes. This may not happen the first time you try, but connecting with other spiritual forces takes a while.

When you feel you have done enough, release these images and energies, even if they haven't been strongly experienced. Give thanks to the tree for sharing, and let yourself relax and draw away. If you aren't able to do this often with your actual tree, try it while lying relaxed in bed, imagining your chosen tree.

Links between Earth and Heaven

Each tree has its own aura, an individual form, a particular smell and a sense of being, created by Nature, shaped by wind and weather. Each tree is a magical link between Earth and Heaven, uniting both in a vegetative harmony. The shade around an individual tree at noon is a magical circle, a ring of cool protection from the Sun's rays, or the patter of raindrops.

A Balancing Exercise

If you can, sit on the ground at the foot of a tree that is special to you. Face north, be still and relax and look outwards. Breathe deeply and slowly. What do you see? That viewpoint is unique to you. It could be an ordinary landscape or garden path. Allow your imagination to show you the way to the past. This could be your own past, images of childhood, youth and later life, what you have achieved and what did not succeed. Cherish the positive thoughts this brings and the faces of people you love, and who love you. Send out and receive warm feelings to Nature, the Earth and the sky, and take enough time to allow positive feelings to come to you. If you have any pain or worries, let them go just for now. Like a morning mist fading after sunrise, let them vanish into thin air. The past has no hold over you unless you choose to cling to the wonders, the joys and the good you have done.

Now move to the opposite side of the tree, facing south and looking at what is in front of you. Try to see what is there and what it might mean to you. In your imagination, create another path that leads to your future. What do you aspire to do? You may have plans and wishes, desires and needs, but none of them can become real unless you are prepared to put in some effort. Yes, you may have problems or hit snags on the way forward but you will find that you have the power or the knowledge to overcome these if you want to. Consider your wishes; are they excessive or built on greed or envy? Would achieving them harm someone else? What do you value in life that will support your aims. Think about this deeply, allow new ideas to arise. These might surprise you for they show you are opening magical gates.

Go and sit on the west side of the tree and observe whether the Sun is setting or that shadows are growing towards you. The tree is the central gnomon of a great sundial and from the west comes the light of memory and release. What can you actually see? Does the view suggest anything to you or remind you of places you have been, people you have met or experiences you have shared with someone? Think too, of what have you learned, about yourself, your body, your mind, and your spiritual being. Recall you connections with all the people around you. You are not alone, and the most magical words you might need to say are 'Please, help me!'. All these ideas add up to the person you have become, with your strengths and weaknesses, and just as the tree stands against the wind, you can stand against difficulties, drawing on this accumulated self-wisdom.

Lastly sit facing east and think about sunrise, new beginnings and potential ideas. Remember each new dawn is the first day of the rest of your life. What can you see before you, both as actual scenery and as aims or plans? This is a heavy matter, so be creative and positive. Imagine the falling leaves of Autumn taking away difficulties or blockages to progress that you wish to discard or have outgrown. Take a few deep breaths and centre, like the tree, feeling your inner roots stretching down into stabilizing earth, and breathe in the healing air and calming solar light. This is a powerful exercise, so take your time, think about what you have experienced and what you would like to do next. Later perhaps record your impressions and insights in your magical diary of all these views from the centre.

Plants and Healing

Not only are trees important, but plants generally have always been used in magical situations because they fill so many roles. They can be eaten as ordinary nourishment, but many have occult or healing properties too. All kinds of plants, from tiny herbs to vast trees, have connections to various Gods, and charms can be made from twigs or leaves, carved or woven. There are thousands of medicinal plants and herbs worldwide, and their uses are becoming more popular as their chemistry as well as their invisible powers, called 'virtue' by old herbalists, are better understood. Traditional healers and witches gathered extensive knowledge of plant powers, passed down through the generations. Roots, flowers, bark, leaves, roots, fungi and stems may be used in potions, teas, incenses and as magical symbols, each connecting to a particular planet or spiritual power.

Many extensive magical and healing herbal books are available, as are mail order suppliers of dried herbs, incenses and individual resins from which you can make up special blends. This is a huge area of study, but utterly fascinating too. Ordinary culinary herbs can be bought dried or as plants from supermarkets and if you repot them they can last for ages. There is also a Victorian 'language of flowers' used in bouquets to send messages to lovers. Magical charms can be as simple as keeping some mint leaves in your wallet to ensure a mint of money, or sage for wisdom. Spending time in garden centres or botanic gardens and getting to know all sorts of plants, herbs and flowers will open up other areas of spiritual connections. Growing things, even indoor pots, can show you the life force, the beauty and the magical spirit of the plant kingdom.

15

THE MAGICAL MIND AND SPELLS

Magical arts require a focused mind, a specific objective and the patience to bring about your will. By changing your awareness of situations through meditation and concentration, effective strategies may be formulated. Not all schemes go to plan. There are strict rules for successful magic working, often expressed in the phrase 'If it harms none, do what you will'. This is not easy, as you must discover your True will! Often practical magic requires ritual actions, perhaps to purify, consecrate and bless a talisman, using the elements of Earth, Water, Fire and Air. It is essential that you can sense that a change has occurred in the talisman you are creating. Magic will be effective if you are sincere.

Magical ritual works on a mental, psychic and spiritual level, as well as a material one. You use real water to purify, and a lit candle to consecrate, while your mind is seeing a vaster picture than the table set before you. It is this dislocation of awareness that is trained through determined mental practice, allowing you to experience the presence of Gods, angels or elemental powers, all of which are 'real' in their own dimensions. If you don't complete your working honestly and with intent, these awakened images can seep into your dreams and waking hours to disrupt your life. They are not evil or harmful, but like power tools in the hands of children, can be disturbing. Never use any technique you don't understand or any that will change other people's lives. Always get permission to act on their behalf.

Handle Magical Arts with Care

The arts of spell-casting, talisman-making and enchantments have been kept secret for centuries because they are powerful tools, in the same way that chainsaws are powerful. Charms need to be handled with care. We don't understand exactly how the various forms of magic work, but by gentle experiment and patience with these time-less arts, new knowledge can be discovered. Through many centuries charms, spells and talismans have been found to bring about what is requested, but they work effectively only for need, not greed. By using the language of correspondences, of colour, scent, number or symbols, the attention of specific energies can be awoken. These work like telephone numbers, connecting with the most useful energy. However, like a phone call, the line may be engaged or the deity unavailable, or you may have a wrong number!

By regular work, the symbol sets which are most effective become well known and create the links between the practitioner and the end result. For hundreds of years these spells have worked. This nor-mally looks like 'coincidence'. Often the desired result may come about in extremely unlikely circumstances. The spell-weaver must be very certain what is required, select the symbols which best cor-respond to that need, choose the correct planetary hour and con-centrate entirely on a successful outcome. Many of the symbols are natural things; flowers or resins from shrubs, natural pebbles, twigs from significant trees all draw on these items' innate magical and spiritual nature, and that helps any magic to work. You cannot dic-tate to unseen beings how a spell will work, only that its objective is clear and that everything possible has been done to set the spell working correctly. Patience is needed, for to move all the factors into the desired position may take time. It is essential to concentrate only on the end result. Then, suddenly, what was needed or requested happens seldom in the way most of us would imagine.

Spells

Theories of Spell-Craft

Spells are words, traditionally spoken, chanted, sung or written, often in an ancient language. Prayers are a form of spell, if they request help from God or a saint. Usually the words are repeated in the form of an incantation, chant, poem, evocation or mantra. This regular sounding can cause a change in consciousness, allowing the spell-weaver to communicate with the invisible. A well-known example is 'Every day, in every way, I am getting better and better', which was used in the nineteenth and early twentieth centuries by French psychologist Emile Coué. Many exercises in self-awareness or to boost confidence involve speaking or singing phrases regularly so that they encourage the subconscious mind towards healing. Mantras used in Eastern meditation may just be letters of the Sanskrit alphabet, but they condition the mind to relax into a meditative state. Repetition is a way of learning as when young children repeat words, songs or nursery rhymes.

In ancient times when writing was seen as a magical act, spells were written and carried about, or the paper was washed and the water drunk as a way of taking in the benefit of the spell. These were made by experts, often for a specific purpose, or sacred texts could be used as an amulet. You can formulate your own spells by choosing a need, and writing a short poem, to inscribe, sing or chant. Keep it specific and direct, and be ready to pay for what you request, and to give sincere thanks when your spell works.

In the Harry Potter books and films by J.K. Rowling, spells are said in Latin. They are too simple to really work, but if chanted three or nine times with intent could prove helpful. 'Accio' means to call or summon, and 'Appareo' makes something appear. 'Finite Incantatem' could be useful to stop another's spell, as could 'Impedimentum', which blocks their effect. However, real, rather than fictional, spells require knowledge of correspondences, planetary movements and symbolism that can't be learned in a school. Today not so many people know Latin or other mystical languages. It always helps to construct your spells in your own language as you can say what you really want, and can tailor them to your exact needs. It is important to know what you are doing.

Modern spells, which act like a phone number, are often in verse as it helps with remembering the words, which should always be said from memory, not read. That is why spell books don't work. A new spell should be written and learned for each situation, working at the right phase of the Moon – waxing to increase something, waning to drive harm away.

The sign of the Zodiac can also influence events, if used properly, but again, this is a deep study. Each sign is associated with an element, Earth, Water, Fire or Air, and can strengthen an appropriate magical action. Traditionally spells draw on the power of the planets. For example, to bring courage or determination, call upon Mars, the red planet. Hold an iron nail and chant five times 'Lord of iron, strength of steel, make your power of courage real.' Wrap the nail in red cloth and chant, 'Mars, empower me with your might, keep my determination tight, that I may act to set things right. So may this be.' Venus brings harmony, Mercury aids communication, Jupiter supports success in career and law-related matters, the Moon assists your mental power, the Sun offers healing and old Saturn grants persistence.

Spells are ended with a statement like 'So mote it be', which means 'may this happen'. Strangely 'Amen' is actually a plea to the ancient Egyptian Sun God AmenRa, which might surprise some Christians!

If a spell fails, don't bother to repeat it. Ask yourself whether what you asked for a wish and not a necessity.

Spell Ethics and Practicalities

Although there are books of spells, these don't often work except for the witch who wrote them. It is far better to consider the underlying factors and spend effort on making your own spell. Any act of magic has to be voluntary, thought through and not directed to anyone without their permission. Only do healing spells if you are asked to, and never try to make someone love you. If they don't already, they never will and this will harm you as it is an area of grey magic. Spells for money won't work either, as cash is an intermediary between the buyer and the purchase. If you need, not want or desire, something, do a spell to get what you really need. Greed or envy are not valid reasons for wanting to possess something. If you need a holiday, ask and you might get an offer from a friend to share or one of your family could invite you to join them on a trip. If you want something for a one-off event consider hire, or swaps or free recycling sites as well. Ask and you may be amazed at what turns up!

Decide your exact objective and consider the ethics of wanting it. Would getting it harm anyone or deprive them of something? Be prepared to do everyday work towards achieving your aim. Choose a power, deity or planet to focus your spell. If you are weaving the spell around an object, either natural, like a stone, or made, like a bag of magical herbs, have these ready. Collect a coloured candle, appropriate incense/joss stick corresponding to your chosen power, and light these before you speak. Write out the words of the spell to bring you exactly what you are asking for then commit them to memory. Traditionally spells were made to rhymes, which needed to be repeated several times. Recite your spell with full concentration and intent. Wrap the enchanted item in clean cloth, ideally silk or cotton, and put somewhere out of sight. Snuff out the candle and tidy up.

Spelling It Out

Spells, like seeds planted in the ground need to be left alone to become effective. This can take a while, days or weeks, but look out for signs that the spell has worked.

Here is a general idea for a spell that can be used for any positive purpose, so adapt it and improve it for your own use:

I speak this spell by Moon and Sun,
I weave this spell: My will be done.
I chant this spell by Sun and Moon,

May what I ask for come quite soon.

I ask (planetary power etc.) to send help to me.
Thank you all. So mote it be!

As another example, here is an idea for a spell to protect your car by
calling upon the planet Mars:

On my machine of glass and steel,
Protective power to me reveal.
Bless this car along the way,
Help me driving's rules obey,
When my car is left alone,
Keep it safe on Earth and Stone.

So may it be.

16

Talismans and Charms

Talismans

Talismans are the most complicated and varied items, each being made for a specific purpose by an expert. They take many forms, from paper and ink to gold studded with diamonds. Each one is dedicated to a particular need, so the symbolism used should be related to that need, and the making will focus all the powers possible on bringing about a good result. Because talismans are made from enduring materials, examples which are many thousands of years old may be seen in museums all over the world. Talismans speak to the unseen powers with the language of symbols, calling for specific help by use of shape, colour, sigil, angelic name and planetary force. To make them effective they are often related to the planets, which act as focusing lenses between the maker and the end result. It is possible to have a talisman made for you by a magician, but ideally you will do some of the work yourself.

A Brief History of Talismans

Ancient talismans were set up as boundary stones, marking the edges of territory, or to prevent wars between neighbours. Examples exist from ancient Assyria and Egypt. Many other examples were designed to bring luck, or attract the attention of a certain God or

SPIRITUAL ECOLOGY

Goddess. Some were placed above or beside doors (such as the Jewish Mezuzah), to keep out unwanted influences. In the folk song 'Green grow the rushes, oh!' five for the symbols at your door refers to pentagrams, the sacred star symbols used by some Pagans, and many door knockers are in the shape of protective talismans.

Even company logos are often based on some magical symbol, Zodiac sign or other success-bringing sign, for example Starbucks' mermaid and stars, or pharmaceutical companies using the staff with a serpent, a symbol of Aesclepius, the Greek God of healing. These magical symbols are all around us once we open our eyes and see.

Basics of Talisman-Making

The most common factors called upon when making talismans are the elements of Earth, Water, Fire and Air. Sometimes Spirit is considered to be the fifth element. The ancient Greeks believed that all matter was made up of these elements in varying proportions. Today physicists consider that everything is made up of particles, waves, energy and plasma, with dark matter or dark energy completing the picture.

Talismans are often created using the powers of the planets, originally considered to be the Sun, the Moon, Venus, Mercury, Mars, Jupiter and Saturn. The earliest written records in all ancient civilizations are of movements of these visible lights in the night sky, naming them as Gods and Goddesses. Each planet has acquired a collection of attributes like metals, colours, angels, incenses, numbers and deities. They are seen to symbolize certain concepts like energy, love, endurance, healing, travel and psychic ability. To us this may seem like superstitious nonsense, but actually these correspondences act as mental keys, or psychic lenses, focusing the magician entirely on the purpose of the talisman, its making, purification and consecration, which sets it to work. The effort of creating a talisman from the correct material, even working in the right planetary hour, bringing together as many correspondences as are relevant, all focus the trained inner parts of the magician's mind on making the talisman a success. There are a great many books devoted to these magical associations.

Basic Table of Planetary Correspondences

Planet	Sort of Magic	Virtue	Colour
Moon	Mind/Dreams	Independence	Silver
Mars	Energy/Action	Courage	Red
Mercury	Communication/ Travel	Honesty	Orange
Jupiter	Career/Law	Obedience	Purple
Venus	Love/Friendship	Generosity	Green
Saturn	Old Age/Patience	Silence	Black
Sun	Health/Self	Devotion	Gold
Earth	Elemental/Crafts	Discrimination	Brown/Green

Planetary Powers

Each of the visible planets is connected to a day of the week, when talismanic work may be done, and associated with a metal, number, incense used to consecrate it, and certain written words or symbols. Learning a long list of correspondences can seem tedious, but it is an essential part of making your own talismans, which are the most effective.

What has to be established is the link between the purpose and the planetary or other powers that are called upon. Once you know which is appropriate, you can pick the best day to work.

- Monday, ruled by the Moon is good for sleep, dreams and inspiration.
- Tuesday, for Mars, when you need energy or an iron will.
- Wednesday is good for communication, perhaps from an out of touch friend when Mercury is called on.
- Thursday rules careers, law and social standing under the stern gaze of Jupiter.
- Matters of the heart, friendship and cooperation are helped by Venus on Fridays.
- Saturday's Saturn benefits long-term plans, old age and time-related projects.

- The Sun is good for health and healing, personal determination and self-confidence on Sunday.

As an example, a statement of 'I wish to sleep more peacefully', signed with your name might be the simplest form of talisman. This should be done on a Monday, after sunset, during a waning Moon. The talisman could be wrapped in silver foil, blessed in moonlight, and a prayer offered to Hypnos, the Greek God of sleep, to grant your desire. Wine, honey or milk could be poured on the ground as an offering, and white flowers should be displayed. Once the talisman is made and blessed it should be hidden in a dark place and forgotten about for one month. Your sleep patterns will improve, if you have acted with concentration and sincerity, and kept quiet about it.

Often one planet may be assisted by the colour, number or shape of another to add an extra dimension of focus to any paper talisman. A blue Jupiter talisman might be written in gold ink and enclosed in a golden envelope. Mars' energy and force might be balanced by co-operating with Venus, using red and green together.

Uses for Talismans

Talismans can be created for all kinds of things, all the time remembering they will be working on a spiritual as well as a physical plane. Always be respectful and mindful of what you are doing. When you make a talisman, consider who is it for. If not yourself, you must have permission to act for someone else, and know exactly what they are asking for. Some magical activities, rituals or talismans can also be aimed at helping Nature and the planet as well as smaller and more local concerns.

Short-term objectives you might wish to create a talisman for could include:

- Getting a new job
- Finding a suitable new home
- Finding a lost object
- Dealing with a legal matter
- Protection on a specific journey

Some of these concepts may have 'green' or spiritual aspects too.

For longer term objectives, enduring talismans can be made in a number of ways to protect yourself or your children throughout their lives or to protect the environment. You can make talismans or recite spells to protect your house or car from burglary or attack, or to keep you from illness. You can request insight, spiritual well-being or guidance as to how to live well, or achieve success or happiness.

Often old spells were designed to bring fertility to farm crops and livestock, or to conceive children and protect them. Traditionally you might ask a blessing from a particular saint, deity or angel to keep you from harm or bring you good luck or to seek inspiration, creativity and harmony in your work. Some talismans are simply for giving thanks, in the way that people put signs in their windows to remember events, say 'thank you' to medical staff or teachers, and even set up roadside shrines when someone has died. A bunch of flowers can be a kind of talisman offering love, hope and wellbeing, if there is feeling behind the gift.

Ways of Making Talismans

Talismans follow traditional formulas, calling upon specific unseen powers like angels, Gods or planetary energies, using symbols to focus the talisman maker's will to bring about the desired result. Every action in making a talisman is part of a process, so needs to be done thoughtfully and with intent. The moment you start to do something, it will become part of the magic so be prepared. You should always consider these questions:

- *Why make a talisman*? What are you aiming to achieve?
- *What will you do when it works?* Often people doubt the validity of magic so never give a thought as to what they will do when the spell or talisman works – think it through. If you are designing it for someone other than yourself, you must have permission to act for them, and know exactly what they are asking for.

- *When is the right time to make it?* A waxing Moon brings increase, whereas a waning Moon decreases something, like an illness or a problem. Each planet has a day of the week, and several hours in each day when it will be most powerful and helpful.
- *Who should you ask for help to bring about the talisman's purpose?* A God/angel/planet or other spiritual being? You have to respectfully acknowledge these are real forces which can have a profound effect of your life.
- *What is the talisman to be made of?* Although historically talismans have been made on wood and stone and the most enduring ones are made with metal, they are only ever intended for one-off use. They should be destroyed once they have worked, or a reason for their not working has been discovered, and so there is no need for them to be made from enduring material. Today simple talismans may be made of thick paper or card in appropriate-coloured ink, or using the planetary symbolism of plants, even leaves, flowers, perfume or bark.

Begin with preparation of a working table with card, pens, wrapping for the finished article, a candle of the corresponding colour and incense/joss sticks and so on. As you progress, you will be able to refine this part of the magical operation, including learning how to get into the right meditative frame of mind. When the talisman has been completed, it will need to be blessed with a request that it will work properly, then it will begin to be powerful. Wrap it and keep it safe while it works.

You could copy this information into your magical diary and add to it as you learn more. Also record any spells or talismans you make. They may not work immediately, but when you look back you could be surprised if what you worked for has happened. Magic doesn't always come out how we expect, so be prepared for the unexpected.

Charms

Charms can be seen as a wide variety of objects, found or manu-
factured, which bring good fortune in a passive way. You may buy,
make or find some object which you believe to be lucky, but once
you have it you only need to carry it around. It could be a miniature
horseshoe, an ancient symbol linked with the Moon and that beneficial animal, the horse, or a cross as a sign of religious conviction. It
could be a lucky scarf at a football match to help your team win, or a
lucky pen for exams; simply having the charm about you is enough.

This passive form of talisman may have been blessed or made
more powerful by coming from its original location, like a pebble
from a healing spring, or sprig of a sacred tree, but it doesn't have
to be adapted or made by the user. Many people pick up interesting
shaped stones or crystals if they find them. Rose quartz is found on
Cornish beaches, jet in East Anglia and garnets in the Scottish high-
lands. Every gem has its links to birth signs and planetary powers
to bring health and wealth. Although the term 'charm' is sometimes
given to spoken words, for example Rudyard Kipling's 'A Charm':

> Take of English earth as much
> As either hand may rightly clutch.
> In the taking of it breathe
> Prayer for all who lie beneath.

Just pick it up to bring success.

Charms You Can Try

One form of charm that requires a little effort is a 'Charm to cure
warts'. This sort of spoken charm was said by a wart-charmer over
the person who wanted his warts cured. This might have been a
chant or incantation, along the lines of 'Wart, wart, black of heart,
I command you to depart'. Many other forms of wart charming
involved rubbing something on to each wart, and burying it to let
it rot and cause the warts to disappear too. Bits of meat, or a live

snail, pieces of string with a knot for each wart, or even coins were touched to each blemish and then cast away. Some wart-charmers even bought warts for a small coin, and touched the afflicted places to draw out the spot. Other old charms include juice of dandelion stems, dabbed on each wart until it goes dark. There are chemicals in the juice which destroy the virus that causes warts.

When we say something is charming we mean it is attractive, but it doesn't mean we want to possess it. We use terms like enchanting, enticing or alluring in respect of objects or people we might be slightly scared of. Fascinating or bewitching, that is the nature of charms; they entice harm away.

Some forms of charming, practised by experts all over the world, relate to animals, such as snake charming or horse whispering. By body language and movement, the wild animal is calmed and encouraged to do what the charmer wants. Now we understand more about how animals think and react, and know that the pipe music doesn't attract the snake, which has no ears, but rather the swaying movement of the charmer which lulls it and makes it seem to dance. By being charming you can often get what you want!

17

UNDERSTANDING DIVINATION AND AN
INTRODUCTION TO THE TAROT

There are a great number of ways of using items to predict the future or explain the human condition. Some of these are traditional like reading tea leaves, or seeing pictures in the fire. Other seers use intuition, psychic sensing and connections with the spiritual world to try to understand certain situations. You can't really learn to be psychic but you can find out you are already sensitive and by practice and opened spiritual awareness develop these skills. Psychology has given us terms for ancient skills, and scientific techniques to examine strange abilities.

Dowsing is a very old art, used to locate water originally but now has been expanded to look for minerals, voids and energy lines, sometimes called leys. Originally a forked hazel or willow stick was used and then simple pendulums were introduced. It is possible for most people to use a pendulum effectively. Any small weight on a string will do and a code of movements for 'Yes' and 'No' are established. Foods, and people with illnesses can be tested to find what is best, and dowsing 'yes/no' can answer questions about all sorts of things.

Tarot Cards as Oracles

For centuries people have sought answers from seers and oracles, or used all sorts of devices from cards to animals' entrails or the flight of birds to show the future. One system which has been popular for several hundred years is the Tarot, a pack of seventy-eight cards with four suits and twenty-two picture cards. There are hundreds of Tarot packs available these days with themes of animals, mythology, fantasy or the Grail Quest, for example.

To learn to get clear information or 'read the Tarot' can take years of study, for every card has multiple meanings. Understanding the images, individually or in set patterns, can offer insights towards knowing yourself and finding inner guidance. There is no magic in the cardboard pictures of the pack, but with intuition and genuine honesty, anyone can get some helpful or insightful information.

The Tarot or similar divination tools cannot predict exactly what is going to happen in the future, but they can reveal aspects of your intentions or the outcome of past actions which have not been clear to you. They can also help you discover solutions to problems with career, family, decision-making and self-confidence. Here is a brief description of how to understand this divining art, but as each Tarot deck is different, each will have its own spirit and direction of thought, and its creator will have had their own interpretations of the cards, described in the accompanying booklet.

Different Uses of the Tarot Cards

Most Tarot packs can be looked at in several ways, but one of the simplest is to see the cards as a kind of universal family photo album, showing images to you throughout your life, from birth, through school, to partnerships, career and friendships. The Tarot reading takes a selection of those images which best correspond to the problem posed or the advice needed. They are not immutable and there are many dilemmas that they cannot address, and aspects of the future that they cannot reveal. They offer some guidance, often, as with most divinatory methods, in oblique or inexact ways.

They give hints, not firm advice, and there is quite a lot of room for personal interpretation.

Often today the Tarot is used as a source of information to meditate on as the pictures can be confusing. Although the earliest packs of cards only date from the fifteenth century, the images they depict are very ancient, occurring in art and sculpture for thousands of years. The most popular decks were published in the early twentieth century, but since then dozens of writers, artists and researchers have devised their own packs on many themes including natural scenes, trees and wild animals, some with more or less than the traditional seventy-eight cards. There are scores of books on these varying systems and most are readily available.

One way to look at the Tarot deck, if you are new to this form of self-help and inner advice, is to see the seventy-eight cards divided into smaller groups. Each traditional Tarot pack has four suits of fourteen cards, plus twenty-two picture cards. Each of the suits has ten 'spot' or number cards as well as four royal cards with images of a King, a Queen, a Knight and a Page. Some decks have images on every card, while others are simpler with numbers of symbols for the spot cards. The suits are usually shown as Wands, Swords, Cups and Pentacles, and there are all sorts of ways to attributing these to the Four Elements used in magical spells. In fact, each card can be a spell or meditation image on its own.

When trying to understand the Tarot as a device for self-exploration it can help to divide a new deck into three sets of cards. This is not the conventional way to master their symbolism, but it can be a way to start. First set aside the Major Arcana or Trumps. These are always picture cards and numbered from zero to twenty-one. Next take each suit of Wands, Swords, Cups and Pentacles and sort out the 'spot' cards (usually ten cards with the Cups, Swords, Wands or Pentacles on them), leaving the Royal set, or the Kings, Queens, Knights and Pages. Different decks of Tarots may call these something else, depending on the theme. These three groups of cards, Trumps, Royalty and spot cards each represent a different aspect of a person's life. The Trumps often represent important people in your life or significant factors, and when seeking advice from the cards can give us direct hint or suggestion.

The Picture Cards

The Royal cards can represent people you know – teachers, friends, relatives, young or old. Without analyzing too much, see if you feel that one card represents a parent, a distant cousin, or young member of your family. Some of these cards show landscapes or horses, for example, and this can indicate distance in either location and travel, or time. As you get to know the cards, the images will speak to you more clearly.

With decks that have pictures on the spot cards, these often show a situation like a challenge or battle; an occupation like a stonemason at work, or an event like a celebration or prize-giving. Other cards can show emotions like sorrow or loss, or joy and success. The author of each deck of cards will have given their Tarot an individual twist, and though many modern packs share similarities, the usual booklet, accompanying the Tarot will indicate the designer's own background or interest. It is sometimes thought that to read the cards you just have to memorize the booklet, but really you need to find your own meaning and interpretation of each image.

The Four Suits

The four suits are often linked to the Four Elements, which are used in the Western esoteric tradition. Earth relates to the physical world, to Nature, to everyday occupations and activities, so the cards each represent someone or something of a practical nature. Water cards are associated with emotion, feelings and experiences, also matters of the heart, friendships, love and romance. Fire cards indicate energy and the way it is used, action and passion, ambition and struggles of various kinds. Air cards are concerned with the mind, with inspiration, which actually means 'breathing in'. The people shown on the cards may be wise folk, teachers or even inner guides rather than physical friends and neighbours.

Pentacles or Coins are often linked with the element Earth and indicate wealth or practical resources, job opportunities or money luck. Luck can run both ways, of course, and gains or losses may be shown. Cups generally indicate matters of the heart or hearth, relationships, love and partnerships of all kinds. They may answer questions about how you feel about a situation. The elements attributed to these two suits are commonly accepted, but when it comes to Swords and Wands there can be different opinions.

To me, Swords relate to fire, for their metal blades cannot be made without smelting ore from rock, shaping it in the forge fire, and what is produced is a weapon of attack or defence. Many blades are in the form of a flame. The Wands seem to be derived from spears or arrows, the first tools for digging edible roots or bringing down game. Considered individually, they may fit different elements, but if the suits are divided into pairs, of Swords/Fire/South and Pentacles (or perhaps Shields) /Earth/North and Cups/Water/West and Wands (or Spears) /Air/East you have two basic situations. Facing East, you would have your Sword in your right hand and your Shield on your left, a position of the Warrior or Defender. If you face North, you have your Wand/Shepherd's crook or Walking Staff in your right hand and your Cup/Wine Glass in your left so you are at home and at peace. You are always at the centre of your own Elemental circle.

Although there are many interpretations of the cards, and hundreds of different sets to choose from, it is worth considering some very basic information on the Tarot. Often people start by looking at the Major Arcana, the twenty-two picture cards that show symbolic images of considerable importance. The following list looks at them in numerical order, although there are variations on this that you might find if you read widely. Cards which show people can indicate a person with the attributes listed, or hidden aspects of your own character.

1. THE FOOL: Innocence, folly and inspiration
2. THE MAGICIAN: Will, skill and problem solving
3. THE HIGH PRIESTESS: Wisdom, memory and practical knowledge

4. THE EMPRESS: Fertility, initiative and mundane authority
5. THE EMPEROR: Willpower, creativity, determination
6. THE HIGH PRIEST: Inspiration, mercy, benificence
7. THE LOVERS: Passion, choice, partnership
8. THE CHARIOT: Triumph, protection, advancement
9. JUSTICE: Balance, honour, a just outcome
10. THE HERMIT: Self-reliance, a beacon, learning
11. THE WHEEL OF FORTUNE: Luck (can be positive or negative), destiny, chance
12. STRENGTH: Force, energy, discipline
13. THE HANGED MAN: A test, self-sacrifice, opportunity
14. DEATH: Completion, sudden change, release
15. TEMPERANCE: Moderation, balance, comparison
16. THE DEVIL: Challenge, ill-health, change
17. LIGHTNING STRUCK TOWER: Deception, revelation, breakdown
18. THE STAR: Hope, light at the end of the tunnel, guidance
19. THE MOON: Vision, be prepared and look out
20. THE SUN: Healing, happiness, success
21. THE LAST JUDGEMENT: Decision, change, completion
22. THE WORLD: Harmony, attainment, goal achieved

If you learn these basic meanings, study the images and the symbolism of each card, you will allow your inner awareness to interpret these for you. Share these divining skills with friends, discussing meanings and interpretations of spread patterns. Gradually, if you ask respectfully, the Spirit of the Tarot will talk to you, and if you listen you will start to gain wisdom

There are many other systems of divination you can work with, but do be patient. These ancient interpretation skills cannot be learned in a day; it can take months or years to master any system. You are building a relationship between your own human spirit and the inspiring spirit of the divinatory medium.

Afterword:
Entering a New World

The Spring of 2020 will be remembered as the time our world was radically altered. The normal freedoms we enjoyed were prevented, many jobs were changed with people working at home, and children's schools and colleges and universities were closed. Our ability to share the companionship of friends, family and loved ones was cruelly curtailed by the pandemic of Covid 19. The whole world and all its peoples found themselves enclosed in their homes, or permitted only a few opportunities to leave the house for certain jobs, essential shopping, or to keep medical appointments. Hospitals struggled to treat astounding numbers of people afflicted by this new and, to some, deadly disease. Every day the death toll increased worldwide, and because of the extreme level of infection and fast spread of this virus, many sick individuals were separated from their loved ones at this critical time. The whole situation caused intense worry, anger and grief to almost everyone, and feelings of helplessness and depression were widespread. However, health authorities, doctors, nurses and all the auxiliary staff never gave up. Experts in virology and vaccine development worked round the clock to find an effective antidote. Manufacturers around the world produced millions of doses, and all sorts of places like sports centres, village halls and city shopping centres became vaccination hubs. New treatment clinics were set up in weeks, and test centres were opened all over the country to help carers, patients and older folk find out if they had or had previously caught this awful virus. Some people escaped the waves of infection, or suffered just a very minor attack, most recovering over time. But both patients and their medical carers still died in large numbers throughout the world. However, the vaccination roll-out saved many lives, and will continue to do so, if populations follow local guidelines.

Overcoming Changes

The extensive changes which swept across the globe fell upon everyone so quickly. Most of us recognize that change happens, which is sometimes for the better, but can be to our detriment. However, Covid was a thunderclap of restriction, of limitation and threat to our wellbeing on so many levels. This has been social evolution in the blink of an eye instead of the gradual shifting of the way things used to be. Our inner selves are used to the regular pattern of day and night, of Spring, Summer, Autumn and Winter, and the waxing and waning of the Moon, but the sudden onset of a pandemic shook the planet to her core. We have been forced to live in new ways, and there is no knowing if things will get back to how they were before 2019.

Although many of the things we normally did were limited, the reduction of traffic on the roads, and far fewer planes flying all allowed the air to be purer, the sky actually bluer on sunny days, and the songs of birds to be heard and not drowned out by mechanical noises. We were also all forced to take a hard look at our lives. What seemed so important and immediate, so ordinary and everyday may have been lost when social contact was forbidden. Standing in the doorway, or in the garden, talking to those nearby may have opened different doors to friendship, companionship and shared experience that we never expected or thought possible.

Most people who were shut in longed to walk in green spaces, or go to the beach, or a holiday destination. The desire to go out into Nature often became paramount. Nature has always been around us. Even in cities gardens, parks and river or coastlines make up

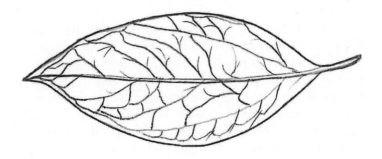

quite a large proportion of the landscape, but before Covid 19 we were able to ignore it and concentrate on the built for what it offered us. During the pandemic many people with gardens tended their plots, planting seeds and mowing grass. Once garden centres and DIY stores reopened, plants, gardening tools and decorating materials were bought in large numbers. More vegetable seeds, plants and containers have filled open spaces, allowing Summer flowers, fruiting trees and herbs to flourish. Gardening in any form, from the simple window box to the wide acres of an estate, has provided fertile soil for the mind as well as for plants and trees. Many people were 'Nature-deficient', especially children. Being outdoors allows our bodies to absorb essential Vitamin D, even on cloudy days, which is vital to our wellbeing. But daylight, unfiltered by a building, is important to our mental and spiritual health too.

Advantages of Creativity

Creativity has also flourished, helping children with their education, making things out of what is to hand, indulging in arts and crafts, and rediscovering forgotten abilities to write and communicate. Of course, high-tech phones and I-pads have helped people stay in touch with friends and family at a safe distance, but many people have found new skills as bloggers and film-makers. Doing any creative activity is valuable as it takes the artist away from the worries and stresses of modern life, allowing their inner selves to shine through.

We may have largely healed people's bodies, but their minds and souls have been damaged by world events and these really do need the gentle touch of inner thought, meditation and magic to be whole again. The pandemic has caused governments to examine their nations' state of health, the general wellbeing of its population, the services of care that need to be overhauled and the medical infrastructure. Education has also come under the spotlight as children were held back from schools to learn at home on screens instead of in class from teachers. Even the subjects they learn is being re-examined and reassessed. A great number of changes to every aspect of life are becoming a new, ongoing reality. Not everything is wonderful or back how it was before, but there is potential for positive change. Perhaps this has been a necessary shift in global consciousness, so we can all realize how fragile our lives and society are. Everyone is offered the opportunity to embrace a fresh interaction with our occupations, our human relationships and how we will live in future.

If we tend to our spiritual needs, as well as our bodily health, we will be better able to tackle the other worldwide crises that beset our planet. Climate change is severely affecting many parts of the world and it isn't going to go away or be fixed by billionaires throwing vast amounts of cash at it. Each one of us should try to tread more lightly on the world, use less energy, drive cars less, eat local, seasonal produce and grow gardens. No one can solve this dilemma alone, but by working together in kindness and thoughtfulness, and drawing on our spiritual links with Mother Nature we may help to turn the tide. Open your inner eyes to the source of life and practise Spiritual Ecology – you will know the magic is real.

Further Reading

These are some of the most useful authors. I am not naming specific books as most of these writers have published a number of titles, and will be producing many more but here are some names and their subjects to conjure with:

Ronald Hutton: books on Witchcraft, Druidry and History of Magic
Rae Beth: books on Hedge Witchcraft
Marian Green: books on Natural Magic, Ritual Techniques and the Quest for the Holy Grail
John Matthews and Caitlin Matthews: books on Shamanism, Celtic Mysteries, Legends and King Arthur
Philip Carr-Gomme: books on English Magic and on Druidism
Val Thomas: books on Norfolk Lore and Magic
Gareth Knight: books on Ritual Magic
Dion Fortune: books on The Qabalah
Doreen Valiente: books on Witchcraft
Sir David Attenborough: books on Nature and Climate Change
Adam Henson: books on Farming Life
H.R.H. Prince Charles: books on Organic Gardening and Country Life.

There are many fiction writers whose works contain real magic, including Terry Pratchett, Ursula Le Guin, Ben Aaronovitch, J.K. Rowling, Christopher Fowler, Alan Garner and Susan Cooper.

RELATED TITLES FROM ROBERT HALE

ISBN 978 0 70904 851 0

ISBN 978 0 70907 383 3

ISBN 978 0 71982 645 0

ISBN 978 0 70906 450 3